Long Road to Dry River

Jennifer Severn

First published by Jennifer Severn in 2019
This edition published in 2019 by Jennifer Severn

Copyright © Jennifer Severn 2019
jennifersevern.com.au
The moral right of the author has been asserted.

All rights reserved. This publication (or any part of it) may not be reproduced or transmitted, copied, stored, distributed or otherwise made available by any person or entity (including Google, Amazon or similar organisations), in any form (electronic, digital, optical, mechanical) or by any means (photocopying, recording, scanning or otherwise) without prior written permission from the publisher.

Long Road to Dry River

EPUB: 9781925786811
POD: 9781925786835

Cover artwork: *Inversion #1* © Rose Chaffey, 2018
Cover design by Red Tally Studios
Thanks to Chumbawamba and EMI Publishing for permission to quote Chumbawamba's 'Tubthumping' in Part Three, Chapter 2.

Publishing services provided by Critical Mass
www.critmassconsulting.com

Some names have been changed.

For Jonathan
14.10.67 – 21.6.2017

and

Naomi Elise
19.7.2017 –

Jennifer Severn grew up in Sydney and has also lived in Melbourne and India.

She's been writing as long as she's been reading. As a child she wrote poems, short stories and book reviews ... no blank piece of paper was safe in her childhood home. She completed a science degree then worked in medical diagnostics and sold medical equipment, later diversifying into jewellery and gemstones. After an MS diagnosis in 1997 she looked for something she could do sitting down and found contract work in technical, scientific and commercial writing before she started a web design business ... and continued to write.

Jennifer's manuscript *Long Road to Dry River* was shortlisted for the Finch Prize for Memoir in 2018.

She lives with her husband and two dogs in Quaama, a small village on the far south coast of NSW, where she still works in web design, volunteers with a community newspaper and writes short stories and non-fiction. You can read her blog at www.jennifersevern.com.au, or follow her on Facebook (DryRiverWritings).

The solicitor's office is small and stuffy and smoky. Light struggles through gappy venetian blinds, faintly illuminating the motes of dust in the air. Ashtrays brim with cigarette butts. Towers of manila folders, some tied with slim pink ribbons, teeter on filing cabinets, on each end of the desk, in every corner on the scuffed linoleum floor.

Across the desk from me, the solicitor is sifting through my file, occasionally stopping to read an entry, and grunting softly. Sometimes he lifts his eyes to peer at me over the top of his spectacles, then returns them to the papers. He's stout and red-faced, and wheezes softly with every breath. From time to time he sips coffee from a chipped china tea cup.

I sit silently and wait. I've driven for two hours down the peninsula from Melbourne on a friend's recommendation. 'He's like a bull terrier with a bone,' my friend had said. 'Just what you need.' Looking around me, I'm beginning to wonder if I've wasted my time. But finally, after twenty minutes, he closes the folder, leans back, clears his throat and says something that floors me.

'D'you think you might've got the MS because you can't forgive your dad?'

Part One

1. some future adventure

'I'm Sukh.'

I had almost dozed off, hypnotised by the rhythmic swish of the wiper blades. 'Sorry?'

'*Sukh*,' said the driver. 'My name's *Sukh*.'

He had sad, brown eyes, messy hair, faded jeans and a thick, denim bushman's shirt, with a string of wooden beads just visible at the collar. I looked down at my own attire. A cashmere jumper and a woollen skirt, kitten-heeled pumps … a short strand of pearls. Standard Medical Rep, circa 1988.

I was twenty-two. I had flown back into Sydney Airport from Melbourne, tired after a hectic sales trip. It was cold and raining hard, and I was pleased to settle into the warm, nicotine- and vinyl-stained air of the cab. I wasn't looking forward to getting home—my boyfriend and I had agreed to separate but he hadn't moved out of our Top Ryde flat yet and the atmosphere was cool.

Sukh? I would have loved to offer a more exotic name, but … 'I'm Jenny. Pleased to meet you'.

We were just turning onto Anzac Parade, and between there and Top Ryde—forty-five minutes' drive—we talked. About the planet, mostly, the environment … We agreed on most things, but he seemed to arrive at his conclusions via avenues of deduction, diversions and detours that my left-brain reasoning didn't follow. I'd never met anyone like him. I still haven't.

He clicked the meter off in the driveway of my block of units. I reluctantly got out of the warm cab and stood in the misting rain as he pulled my suitcase from the boot.

He looked sideways for a moment then turned back to me and grinned.

'Well, goodbye, then,' he said. We shook hands shyly. I would enjoy the memory of this taxi ride with Sukh, the erudite and handsome driver, but for now I had to face Simon.

When I got upstairs, I found that Simon had eaten the pasta sauce I'd left in the freezer ready to warm up, and was sitting, stony-faced, in front of *Family Feud*. But there was no point in an argument. I took a deep breath, grabbed my purse and ran back down the stairs, my thoughts on a burrito from Pancho's Grill across the road.

When I reached the ground floor I could make out someone at the security door across the foyer, banging on the glass with the palms of both hands. *Some lowlife for number eleven*, I thought. Then I heard our phone ringing and ran back up the stairs in case it was for me. It was my best friend, Elise, who knew I was due back that night. When I went back downstairs ten minutes later I was glad to see that the 'lowlife' had gone.

A few mornings later I was on my way down to the garage when I noticed a blue airmail envelope tacked to the noticeboard on the ground floor. 'This letter is addressed to Jenny,' the envelope read, 'a gorgeous blue-eyed honey who lives somewhere in this apartment block and whom I chanced to meet once. I would be very grateful if you could hand it to her personally. Thank you. Clue: she works for a medical instrument company.' I tore it open.

Inside were three crisp, sky-blue pages. 'I was driving a taxicab last Wednesday night and picked up a passenger from the Australian Airlines Terminal in Mascot ... On arriving at your destination I was sorely tempted to invite you for a cup of tea or perhaps some future adventure but sadly I held back and drove away rather stunned. I returned shortly afterwards determined to press every intercom button, no matter how foolish, in order that I might speak to you once again'. So the 'lowlife' was him! Sukh! ... I read on.

He supposed I might see his actions as 'pretty foolish, crazy or mad', and wrote, 'life is to be lived and to be crazy is to be alive and to surround one's self with crazy laughing loving dancing trusting sensitive people is a very rare benediction in this world. As I thirst for life, love and laughter, silence and meditation, I must take this small risk that you have in your hand ... Anyhow, if this has reached you and it feels good to read, please phone me to say hello, or leave a message'. He signed off with a phone number.

Some future adventure? A cup of tea? I'd been chatted up before but this was something else.

Simon and I had prided ourselves on being sensible. We'd studied hard and set up life insurance and superannuation policies. We'd done everything possible to remove risk from our lives after the scary, uncertain family lives we'd both left behind. Now, here was a man who appeared to embody the very antithesis of that—crazy, adventurous, risk-taking. *Alive*. I was filled with a sense of living on the edge. I folded up the letter and kept it with me for the next week or so, taking it out to re-read it now and then, and each time feeling the same sense of possibility.

One night, from a hotel room in Newcastle, I rang Sukh's number. A few nights later we had dinner in

Long Road to Dry River

a small vegetarian restaurant in Bondi Junction, and soon we were spending weekends together. Over the next few months Sukh introduced me to seedy pool rooms in Surry Hills; breakfast at cafés on Bondi Beach; share houses full of people with Indian names who slept on futon mattresses on the floor and drank herbal teas; and, last but not at all least, the strange, physical meditations taught by Bhagwan Sri Rajneesh.

He also took me camping in the Blue Mountains.

Sukh and I drive from Bondi out to Blackheath at dawn, turn left across the train tracks and park at a property where the owner's happy for bushwalkers to cross his land. We swing each gate closed as we cross the farm, then midmorning we squeeze through the fence which

holds back the forest, at a point where a ridge juts out towards the Cox River. Here, propelled by the weight of our backpacks, we plunge down the steep escarpment, lurching from tree to tree for handholds, our boots finding purchase on roots and rocks, until we burst out onto a grassy flat beside the water.

The river roars and, where it stills in rocky pools near the banks, is as clear as glass. We hop from rock to rock—pink granite and sandstone. Out there on the river we can sing and shout and not hear ourselves, the torrent's so strong.

On our first weekend in the mountains, Sukh grinned and pointed to my fists; they were clenched tight and I pumped them as I walked. I hadn't been aware of it. I practised swinging my arms, fingers loose. It took a while but eventually I started to feel the breeze on my palms—the chill, eucalypt-infused air of the Megalong Valley.

* * *

Next thing I knew, I'd given notice on the flat in Top Ryde (Simon had moved out) and moved into a big share house in Strickland Street, Rose Bay with Sukh and others, mostly followers of Rajneesh—sannyasins, commonly known as Orange People after the clothes they'd worn in earlier years. Our house was the centre of activities for the local sannyas population, with a huge room perfect for group meditations—and parties. At any one time there would be about eight residents living in the house, and there could be as many visitors camping on landings or in the meditation room.

Our fellow residents were mostly Germans (the house was known in the sannyas community as 'Stricklandstrasse') applying for their Australian permanent residency permits, and there were interminable 'house meetings' where we—well, really the Germans—tried to orchestrate the house's domestic requirements and events (parties, meditations, therapy groups). It was in Stricklandstrasse that I first heard of 'deep cleaning'. This went well beyond spring cleaning. The whole house was dusted, de-cobwebbed, vacuumed, scrubbed, polished ... and a lot more often than this mere Australian would have thought necessary.

One domineering fräulein had appointed herself as a kind of 'houseparent'. If I ever questioned a decision she would glare at me, hands on hips. 'Listen now, oi hef been in ze communes for ten years!' It was common for sannyasins to live in big, co-operative dwellings, but she made them sound like salt mines. And the ones in Germany ... well, I can only imagine the authoritarian hierarchies in those ones.

I suspect now that Sukh and I had landed in the midst of a people processing inter-generational guilt from a war that was over before they were even born.

On that note ... our housemate Swarna, from Berlin, had adopted a young German shepherd pup. He used to wander, and Swarna could often be heard calling him from our rooftop balcony. Ignorant of the meaning—just liking the sound of the word—she'd named the dog 'Shalom', Hebrew for 'peace'. And as she called him from our vantage point on the hill, across the rooftops of the very Jewish enclave of Rose Bay, all the way down to New South Head Road on the harbour foreshore, people could be seen emerging from their doors, waving back and calling 'Shalom! Shalom!' and my head would spin with the levels of irony. The poor dog wouldn't be home for hours.

But Stricklandstrasse wasn't all hand-wringing over bathroom mould and food kitty discrepancies. There was always music playing; tantalising aromas wafted from the kitchen—trays of cheesy vegetarian lasagne, or vats of spicy bean dishes. There were always some housemates wanting to 'hang out', drink tea and chat, and others wanting to 'take their space'—always solemnly respected. I tried smoking dope and gave away my staple drink, the Black Russian. I started using the sweet, lilting 'Na du?' instead of the broad, flat 'How ya goin'?'

Long Road to Dry River

I got used to people walking around the house in varying stages of undress. The upstairs bathroom had two basins, a shower, a bath tub and a toilet, and often in the morning all would be in use at once. I soon dispensed with my prudish self and stepped bravely into this new life. And every weekday morning I'd don my pencil skirts, padded shoulders and pumps, apply eye make-up and lipstick (a process that fascinated Sukh, as did my insistence on wearing a bra) and drive across the Sydney Harbour Bridge to Crows Nest. I'd climb the stairs to the Inmed office, call potential customers, make polite chitchat with my boss and the receptionist, and set out to trawl the cardiac wards and intensive care units of major public hospitals to spruik my product to grim, distracted doctors, with all the enthusiasm I could muster. I was living parallel lives.

* * *

Throughout Stricklandstrasse hung large portraits of Bhagwan—a compelling and complex presence with his deep, hooded eyes and flowing, grey beard, and often a hint of humour around his cheeks, or in the arch of an eyebrow—and his books occupied a shelf in the lounge room. Flicking idly through a 'darshan diary' one Sunday in October, I found the following words.

> The moment you cross the boundary of the known, fear arises, because now you will be ignorant, now you will not know what to do, what not to do. Now you will not be so sure of yourself, now mistakes can be committed; you can go astray. That is the fear that keeps people tethered to the known, and once a person is tethered to the known he is dead.
>
> Life can only be lived dangerously—there is no other way to live it. It is only through danger that life attains to maturity, growth. One needs to be an adventurer, always ready to risk the known for the unknown. That's what sannyas is all about. But once one has tasted the joys of freedom and fearlessness, one never repents because then one knows what it means to live at the optimum. Then one knows what it means to burn the torch from both ends together. And even a single moment of that intensity is more gratifying than the whole eternity of mediocre living.

Bhagwan didn't 'write' books as such but all his words were transcribed by his sannyasins into a vast library of publications. The 'darshan diaries' recorded Bhagwan's conversations with his disciples. In this diary, *The Tongue-Tip Taste of Tao*, he was initiating disciples in Buddha Hall in his ashram in Pune, India—the disciples were 'taking sannyas'. Bhagwan would give each one a new name, and explain what the name meant for their spiritual path. 'Sukh', I learned, meant 'bliss', although it came out more as 'bless' in his Kiwi accent. His full sannyas name was Prem Sukh—'the bliss of love'.

The book was illustrated with black and white photographs of these meetings: Bhagwan holding his thumb to the foreheads of his disciples (the 'third eye', supposed to perceive more deeply than regular sight); Bhagwan placing a string of wooden beads (a mala) over a disciple's head; disciples in flowing robes sitting cross-legged, listening to Bhagwan with clear adoration.

Freedom, fearlessness, adventure ... the known and the unknown ... freedom to make mistakes ... against my safe, sensible, mediocre life. The next day I went to work, handed in my resignation and started making plans.

2. Orphan Annie and the Ice Princess

While I'd launched myself straight into university after school, my best friend Elise had spent a season skiing and cleaning lodges in the Snowy Mountains before completing a degree in Mandarin at Sydney University. Then she'd travelled to China to study, improve her language skills and work. She was very excited to hear, at the end of 1988, that I was planning to travel at last. She suggested meeting up in Hong Kong, an 'easy landing', she said, for someone who'd never been out of Australia (she didn't warn me about the hair-raising descent that planes took to the old airstrip in those days, between banks of laundry-decked skyscrapers that felt only a wingtip away).

We spent a week exploring the hectic markets of the Hong Kong mainland and the downtown of

Hong Kong Island, returning each night to our bunks in a low-ceilinged, windowless dormitory room on an upper level of Chungking Mansions in Kowloon, a popular backpacker accommodation. We weren't aware that earlier that year there'd been a fire in that same high-rise complex—a Danish tourist was killed. I shudder now to imagine residents trying to flee its upper floors via its two creaky elevators and seventeen storeys of stairwells.

When we'd tired of sweating our way through Kowloon's chaotic, steamy alleyways and were craving some nature, we caught the ferry to Lantau Island, at the time a relative wilderness ringed with fishing villages (now the site of Hong Kong's new airport, and connected by a bridge to the mainland). There we spent a week at Po Lin Monastery, which perched atop the highest peak on the mountainous isle, after meeting a monk on a bus who promised us 'lotus pizza' for dinner.

* * *

Next we flew to Thailand. We caught the train north and went trekking in the jungles of the infamous Golden Triangle. Our small party awoke from a late afternoon nap one day, surprised to see our guides transformed from amiable, often comical, young trekkers to furrow-browed security guards, complete

Elise and Jen trekking in Thailand

with semi-automatic weapons. Apparently there'd been a hint of drug runners in the area and our guys weren't taking any chances—kidnappings of moneyed Western tourists were not unheard of at the time. We returned to Chiang Mai unharmed, bought silly trinkets and pirated cassettes for our Walkmans at the night markets, then caught the train back south to drink coconut water and eat banana pancakes and fish slow-baked in deep sandpits on the tropical island of Koh Phan Gan.

I loved being in Asia—the constant bustle, the raucous conversations in the street, the endless energy. I soon learned to love the Asian disregard for personal space—or, a different interpretation of personal space—a world away from the shy, apologetic dance of Australian public encounters. I devoured the food and reached a healthy weight for the first time in many years, perhaps ever.

Back in Bangkok, on the backpackers' mecca of Khao San Road, a huge street party for New Year's Eve was under way. I noticed a long-haired man, his wooden beads swinging wildly as he danced. I grabbed his sleeve. 'You're a sannyasin!'

'Yeah! I've just come from Pune to sort out my visa.'

'I'm going to Pune next,' I gushed. *Where did that come from?* I'd booked a flight to India, but planned to backpack around the country—the route already traced out in my Lonely Planet guidebook—and end my Indian sojourn in Pune. But seeing this man and his mala I felt a longing, almost a homesickness, to again be around the sannyas way of life. Soon I was back in the air, heading further west.

* * *

People ask me what sannyas is. Is it a cult? A religion? A belief system?

I'll start with the last one. That's easy. No. No-one is asked to believe anything. The one thing Bhagwan (or Osho, as he was known by the time he died) stressed was the benefit of meditation. He urged us 'to live life in its totality, but with an absolute condition, categorical condition: and that condition is awareness, meditation'. And even mainstream, conservative scientists have now demonstrated quantifiable, beneficial effects on the brains of meditators.

Is sannyas a religion? Again, no. There's no supernatural figurehead, no-one to worship.

A cult? Wikipedia says, '… a cult is a religious or social group with socially deviant or novel beliefs and practices'.

There's hardly anything deviant or novel about meditation. But Bhagwan said that sex was a distraction to be transcended, and the only way to do that was to experience it fully, with no inhibitions, no fears. So, yes, there was plenty of sex. Or, as much as anyone wanted. But from what I could see it was plain, healthy sex between consenting adults, and it didn't feel deviant to me.

Cults seem to be characterised by the control that a leader exerts over his or her followers. And I saw no sign of control in the ashram in Pune, or in communities I experienced around the world. No rules about where or how to live, conduct relationships, earn a living. We were, are, free to pursue our own goals, make our own mistakes, learn our own lessons. Bhagwan said,

> Always remember, whatsoever I say to you, you can take it in two ways. You can simply take it on my authority:

"Osho says so, it must be true" – then you will suffer, then you will not grow. Whatsoever I say, listen to it, try to understand it, implement it in your life, see how it works, and then come to your own conclusions.

* * *

So I flew out of Bangkok a few days after New Year 1989 and landed in Bombay (now Mumbai) at two o'clock one morning. At the airport a skinny hustler spotted this young, tired tourist.

'Hottle, madam? Very cheap, very comfort!'

I gave him my backpack and followed him to an auto-rickshaw. After a short ride through dimly-lit streets, he led me through a maze of back alleys and cramped courtyards until depositing me and my backpack at a reception desk in a shabby guest-house. I managed to get a few fitful hours' sleep in a cupboard-sized room, water pipes clanging in a cavity behind my pillow, then found my way to Victoria Terminus and bought a second-class train ticket to Pune.

Although Pune was only 150 kilometres east of Bombay, the trip took five hours, most of it stop-start shunting. I shared a compartment with about ten other passengers, all Indians, and immediately found myself the subject of a passionate but amiable debate: I must learn the local language, they told me, but half of them spoke Hindi and half Marathi (the native language of Maharashtra state). Luckily for me, English is almost everyone's second language in India, so it was in English that the good-natured argument proceeded. At every stop, platform food and drink hawkers thrust their wares through the metal bars on the train windows, and my hosts—as they seemed to view themselves—filled my lap with namkeen (paper packets of salty snacks), vegetable 'cutlets' (fried patties) and cups of sweet, milky chai. When we reached Pune they all bid me hearty farewells, their hands pressed together, prayer-like, at the chest. I heaved myself and my backpack off the train, flushed with achievement: I could count to ten in both languages.

The Hotel Kapila in Pune had cashed in on the sannyasin market by partitioning off the top floor with cardboard-thin walls to form monk-like cells just large enough for a narrow single cot and a metal locker. These low-rent rooms were not the place for a good night's sleep after Bhagwan's evening lecture, when the occupants and their partners for the night would arrive in a convoy of rickshaws and fling themselves into noisy and exuberant sex, every detail shared with the neighbours. It was into this haven of lust and unfettered passion that I arrived, tired, dusty and sweaty, to spend my second sleepless night in India.

The next morning, bleary-eyed, I caught a rickshaw—'Ashram, madam?'—and fronted up at the Rajneeshdham reception. I filled in some forms and let a nurse take some blood—everyone entering the ashram in Pune had to have an AIDS test. The results would be available overnight. In the meantime, I caught a rickshaw into town to look around. I was acclimatising to the dust and noise and frenetic activity of India. It was relentlessly alive, and I loved it.

But when I received my ashram pass the next day and entered the gates, I found another world: paths of polished stone meandering between gardens of lush foliage; ponds with waterlilies and swans; a canopy of towering bamboos and ferns and tropical trees casting dappled light on the ground. Even the air was clearer, and a few degrees cooler. Everywhere were the sounds of trickling water and soft music—the breathy flutes and faint tabla rhythms of Indian classical music. Westerners drifted along the paths, or sat on low marble walls chatting.

Wandering further in, I found cafeterias, a bookshop, a vast, marble-floored, open-air meditation space—Buddha Hall, insect-netted all around. More paths, more gardens, all immaculately kept. People were sweeping the paths and tending the gardens. A sound like a loud cat's miaow turned my head: a peacock on a rock in a lotus-filled pond. And all under a soft, filtered light, a world away from the dry dust, heat and commotion of the streets outside.

After a few days I found a room in a shared flat at the 'Popular Heights' apartment complex just a short walk from the ashram, and bought some furnishings: a coconut-fibre mattress, some sheets, a mosquito net and a rack to hang clothes on. At first I tried some 'groups'—therapeutic courses all aiming to dispense with my 'conditioning'. A typical group would see us sit in a circle of eight to twelve, or in pairs, taking part in exercises designed to reveal those subtle lessons that we'd absorbed with our upbringing that were holding us back from being happy and fulfilled. Some exercises were fun, some confronting, some downright frightening. At times I was aware of wanting to show that I was letting go of my conditioning even when I wasn't, just so the facilitators' focus might move to the next person. Sometimes I didn't even *want* to drop my conditioning. I was often confused.

Every night hundreds of visitors from all over the world—German, American, French, Italian, British, Australian, Japanese—filed into Buddha Hall to watch video reruns of Bhagwan's lectures. Bhagwan lived in a house on the perimeter of the ashram, but at the time he was ill and unable to appear in person.

But if the general ashram population was a rainbow of nationalities, it seemed that every therapy group I enrolled in was facilitated by an officious Swiss-German woman who issued instructions like commands from the Gestapo. Role playing was a common device. *Zis man ist your fazzer! Vot do you vont to say to him?* Or, *Zis vooman, she ist your mozzer! Tell her! Tell her!* The German group participants (always a majority) seemed to hold a bottomless well of vitriol in their bellies, and they could unleash it at will. But I would cower, trying in vain to summon the anger that the facilitator—and I—believed I should be feeling. I just couldn't seem to locate it. The facilitator would say I was conditioned to repress my fury. But was it possible that I just wasn't the angry type? Instead, I usually just curled up in tears of frustration and defeat. After the final session disbanded and the group hugs were finished, I'd wander off feeling a sense of failure.

* * *

And I said there was plenty of sex, or as much as anyone wanted. Sukh had encouraged—exhorted!—me to have lovers and experience Pune to the fullest, but I found myself unable to participate with wild abandon. I veered between neediness—wanting to attach myself to someone safe, and punishment—wreaking vengeance on men for sharing a gender with Dad. The only wild bit was the constant crunching gear changes between Orphan Annie and the Ice Princess.

3. no more mediocrity

I tried just hanging out at the ashram, but I found it difficult to be aimless. I think I was bored. Needing to be of use and exercise my analytical brain were clearly aspects of my conditioning that I hadn't yet transcended, because one day when I saw a small sign on the noticeboard, 'Microbiologist needed—enquire with Amiten at the Hygiene Department', I was excited and relieved. I saw the possibility of a way I could stay here—and stay interested.

Amiten was a small, bespectacled Scottish microbiologist who'd been in charge of testing the ashram's food and water. In the land of 'Delhi belly', the objective of the Hygiene Department was to ensure that Western visitors could eat and drink and not fall prey to gastric ailments. Amiten collected samples of food from the ashram cafeterias, and water from the various bottle-filling stations—and even surreptitious specimens of korma, vindaloo and ice-cream from the restaurants and hotels of Pune, just to keep a check on them (the five-star establishments were apparently the most pathogen-ridden, with their bains-marie and salad bars). Then he would process the samples in the ashram's rudimentary laboratory, plate them up on petri dishes and incubate them, inspecting them over the following days and reporting on any colonies of bacteria appearing on the agar gel surfaces.

But Amiten needed to get back to Aberdeen so he was delighted to meet me, trained microbiologists being thin on the ground in the ashram. There was just one hitch—I wasn't a sannyasin, and only sannyasins could be ashram workers.

Most people in the ashram were there for only a few weeks and were focused on groups or meditations or discourses. Longer stayers often signed up to work—there were advantages, such as a food pass for free meals. Workers in the ashram were expected to work (in the kitchens, the gardens, the offices ...) six hours a day, every day, which still allowed plenty of time for meditation.

I'd thought about taking sannyas, but I hadn't felt any need to rush. I could do groups and eat in the ashram cafés and attend meditations and videos in Buddha Hall, and there'd been no pressure to take sannyas. But here was a clear signal. I wanted to work in the Hygiene lab. It felt like a way to 'ground' me in Pune, to give me a purpose apart from the internal investigations that were happening for me.

I signed up to take sannyas.

It was winter—peak time at Rajneeshdham—and there was a backlog of people waiting for their sannyas initiation. After a couple of weeks my day arrived, and all the friends I'd made in therapy groups and around the ashram accompanied me to Buddha Hall, bringing flowers.

There were perhaps ten of us taking sannyas that day. To the side, musicians were riffing on guitars, bamboo flutes and other Indian instruments—soft, melodic music. There was much laughter, and an atmosphere of joy and affection.

* * *

One of Bhagwan's oldest disciples was sitting cross-legged on a cushion on the marble floor. When my turn came I sat on another cushion in front of this warm, smiling woman, buzzing with anticipation. She draped a new mala, with its locket framing Bhagwan's face, around my neck, then handed me a certificate. I read my new name, 'Marga Sahi', and its translation: 'the authentic way'. Then she leaned forward, grabbed my feet and pulled them against her

belly. I felt a jolt of energy enter my soles and shoot up my legs. I shrieked, then laughed out loud. With a smile she waved me away and I wandered over to be enveloped in hugs from my friends. I walked out of Buddha Hall with an armful of flowers and a new sense of anticipation and excitement about this new world I was entering. I tried my new name aloud: 'Marga Sahi'. Just 'Sahi' would do. *Authentic.* Most sannyasins only use the second part of their two-word names.

I suspect that, for me, taking sannyas was partly a quest to belong to something—anything—in a way that I'd never felt I belonged to my family. I'd explored the Christian church in my teenage years, probably for the same reason. In Pune I met a man who'd chanced upon Bhagwan's writings in a secondhand shop in Melbourne, and had booked a flight to India that day. Another had attended a group meditation in a council hall in Birmingham, demanded to know the origin of the instructional cassette that had been playing, and did much the same. I asked a friend once if I was a real sannyasin—I felt my motivation to be shallow in comparison. 'Bhagwan has a hundred ways of drawing his people to him,' she said.

Shortly after I took sannyas, Bhagwan regained his health and returned nightly to Buddha Hall to address his followers. As a worker, I secured a seat near the front on the first night. We all sat on cushions on the marble floor. A small group of musicians was playing traditional Indian instruments beside a low dais at the front, accompanied by crickets, frogs and the rest of the ashram's evening chorus. There was a low, deep armchair on the dais.

Then Bhagwan appeared from a side entrance, his hands pressed together at his chin in the *namaste* greeting. He wore an elaborate robe and a beanie-like knitted cap. Everyone in the hall fell silent and returned the *namaste*.

Walking slowly from one end of the dais to the other, smiling gently with hands folded, Bhagwan appeared monolithic—I was surprised, some time later, to see a photo of him standing in a group of people—he was not a tall man at all. Then he sat on the armchair and started to speak. He read a Zen koan, a kind of Buddhist riddle, then explained it. He spoke for about three hours that night.

Yes, I might have asked for sannyas initiation so that I could work in the Hygiene Lab and cement my sense of belonging in the ashram. On the sannyas spectrum, from rusted-on devotee to casual, good-time seeker, I probably scored towards the latter end. But when Sukh, who'd arrived in Pune in the meantime, met me outside the Hall after that first discourse, he found me almost catatonic, wide-eyed and speechless, unable to explain my response. He just shook his head knowingly and laughed. We spent the night in silence.

* * *

Sukh had commitments and soon returned home, and I continued my routine: my work in the Hygiene lab, meditations and discourses in Buddha Hall, and immersing myself in the frenetic, noisy colour of Mahatma Gandhi Road in central Pune in my free time. But even with my worker's food-pass I was running out of funds. In July I returned to Sydney and Stricklandstrasse, and found a job selling recycled rag stationery to newsagents and gift shops.

In December Sukh and I flew to New Zealand and spent six weeks hitch-hiking and camping the length of the country. One day we set up camp on the bank of the river at Greymouth on the west coast of South Island. We hired two aged but pretty watertight kayaks from the campground manager and soon were happily paddling up a pretty inlet. But we'd misjudged the tides. As the light started to fade and we turned around, we found ourselves battling a strong incoming current. It was impossible to make any headway on the water and we resorted to wading in the shallows, towing the kayaks behind us. Sukh was managing, but I found myself overcome with an all-consuming weariness I'd never known. It was just a leaky kayak but it could have been the Manly ferry I was dragging down that inlet, with cement boots on. I had to stop frequently, and it was only Sukh's increasingly frantic urging that prevented me curling up and going to sleep on the bank.

Eventually we made it back to camp just on nightfall. I collapsed, exhausted. Sukh was setting a fire with some twigs and a newspaper he'd found in a bin when he froze and wordlessly passed me a page he'd been about to screw up and burn. In the margin was a brief item with the headline, 'Free sex guru cremated'.

I roused myself and we trudged a kilometre into town, found a phone box and rang home. I expected weeping and wailing, but sounds of music and laughter came over the line—the Sydney sannyas community had converged on Stricklandstrasse and Bhagwan's (now Osho's) life was being celebrated. Yes, there were tears, but there was also joy.

He'd said, 'If a person lives his life without any fear, authentically, spontaneously, death will not create any fear in him, not at all. In fact, death will come as a great rest. Death will come as the ultimate flowering of life. He will be able to enjoy death too; he will be able to celebrate death too.'

He'd said, 'Death is not the end but the culmination, the crescendo.'

He'd said, 'Ah ... *this* ...'

That night, back at the campsite, I wrote a poem.

> Stunned into silence
> Far deeper than ever by his words
> As our beloved master demonstrates
> Perfectly
> For us
> The ultimate let-go ...
> And then, from somewhere, the laughter arises ...

* * *

When we returned to Stricklandstrasse we found that there was a new German resident, Helmut—tall, blond and with a whiff of criminality about him. Helmut was keen to gain permanent residency, like all the other Germans in the house, and he had money.

He offered me $3000 to help him apply on the basis of a scam de facto relationship.

I was broke and needed a car. Helmut's plan was the solution to my problems—I hardly gave it a second thought. We talked long into the night, memorising each other's habits, hobbies, preferences, intimate details—yes, apparently he was circumcised. Then, one visit to the Immigration Department in the city and Helmut's application was launched. By now I was fully living Bhagwan's words about risk-taking—or my interpretation of them.

We'd hardly submitted the paperwork when I was offered a six-month job in Amsterdam looking after the business of a friend of Swarna's, while the friend and his partner were in Bali for the birth of their child. I'd never been to Europe and leapt at the chance—after checking with Helmut that it wouldn't affect his application (no, but a few lovesick letters home, he said, would be appreciated). I arrived in Amsterdam in March 1990, twenty-four years of age with my own apartment, the top two floors of a converted sixteenth century warehouse on a canal just off the red-light district. I had the use of a car but I also bought myself a rickety fixed-gear bicycle, one of the type readily available on any Amsterdam street corner for about twenty dollars—junkies would steal them and resell them in a high-turnover market. After quickly losing my first bike I also bought myself a good bike lock for about a hundred dollars, for the convenience of knowing my bike would still be where I left it when I got back. I spent many twilight hours cycling along the old city's canals and cobble-stoned streets.

In Amsterdam I met some sannyasins who'd taken a lease on a castle near Stuttgart in the south of Germany. I often drove out of Amsterdam on a Friday afternoon, turned onto the autobahn just over the German border and made it to 'Der Lustschloss' by midnight—the stronghold had been dubbed 'the Lust Castle' in the early nineteenth century when it was reputed to have been the residence of a consort of Napoleon's. We snorted cocaine, we hit the discos in Stuttgart, we wandered the castle grounds stoned, startling the resident herd of spotted deer. One day (quite sober) I borrowed my friend's Porsche 928S, ostensibly to buy him a pack of cigarettes in the nearest village. I got back four hours later after driving to Frankfurt and back on the autobahn, proud to report that I'd topped 220 kph. I was young, I was wild. No more mediocrity: I'd read *The Tongue-Tip Taste of Tao* and I was tasting 'the joys of freedom and fearlessness'. I was determined 'to burn the torch from both ends together'.

* * *

Long Road to Dry River

That September, I was on BA12 approaching Sydney. We were about to descend when the hostie appeared at my elbow, smiling and crouching as they do. She gave me a form, saying that British Airways liked to conduct random surveys of their passengers. Today, it seemed, I was it.

I was a bit spooked. Swarna had called me in Amsterdam just before I left, saying that Interpol had come to the door asking for my 'de facto' Helmut; he'd hightailed it over the back fence and hadn't been seen since. She also said that the house phone might be tapped (she was calling from another house) and that I shouldn't bring address books or any other sensitive items back in my luggage.

I came through Immigration trying to look cool and calm. At Customs they directed me to the Red Lane. The officer went through my luggage, unrolling every sock, sniffing my teabags. It took an hour to get through. Swarna and another friend, Keshava, were in the Arrivals Hall to meet me and I'd just started to relax when two plain clothes cops approached Keshava. They asked to see his ID—maybe they thought he was Helmut. He smiled and showed them his driver's license. He lent them a pen so they could write his name down.

Keshava drove us to a flat on Parsley Bay, Vaucluse, which I was to share with Swarna. I realised that this had all been arranged since the Interpol visit. But after a couple of days one of my former Stricklandstrasse housemates rang me from a public phone. He said that the cops had staked out the house, awaiting my return. He asked me to call them and make my whereabouts known, as they'd threatened to bust the household for growing hydroponic cannabis in a walk-in wardrobe. So I went to a public phone in Vaucluse and rang the number on a card that one of the federal agents at the airport had given me. The officer who answered asked me to hold the line for a minute while he found a pen (did these guys never have pens?), but I hung up and called back after a few minutes. This time he had a pen and we made an appointment for an interview the next day.

Keshava had a neighbour who was a lawyer and I met him in his office in Martin Place. Mikhail was tall, dark and lean with soulful brown eyes. We walked down Elizabeth Street to the Federal Police headquarters. The interview didn't take long—I hadn't been involved in Helmut's alleged activities and I didn't know where he was. I promised to let them know if he got in touch, but I think we all knew that he wouldn't.

On the way down in the lift Mikhail asked me if I'd like to get a coffee.

I hadn't seen Sukh since I'd got back. I heard that he'd holed himself up in Stricklandstrasse, unnerved by the police presence in the street. And Amsterdam had changed me; worldly and cool, I was no longer the starry-eyed sales rep he'd picked up at the airport two years earlier. Ice Princess to the fore. That weekend Mikhail and I were in his car, heading out to the Blue Mountains for a camping trip. I was flicking through the *Sun Herald* and came across a double-page feature article on Helmut, with a mug shot. I closed the paper with a shiver. Or maybe it was more a *frisson*—this was my world now.

The following week Mum rang—she'd read the story. 'It said he lived on Strickland Street, Jen. Did you ever see him around?'

'Mum, he was a criminal. He would have been keeping a low profile.'

'And he had an Australian girlfriend …'

'Yes, so I read!'

There were aspects of my life Mum just didn't need to know about.

***

For the next year I lived in the sunny little flat on the low cliffs of Parsley Bay, Vaucluse, where salty spray speckled the louvre windows when the tide was high. Swarna and I partied hard. I was running a small business with Keshava importing environmental products, a spin-off from my time in Amsterdam, and Swarna was studying fashion design at East

Sydney Tech. We were young and had great clothes. We didn't seem to need any sleep. I was in a passionate, tumultuous liaison with Mikhail, and Swarna had her own rocky relationship. We'd console each other with endless cups of sweet, milky rooibos tea, often meeting Keshava at Speedos Café on Ramsgate Avenue, Bondi Beach.

Mikhail rented a flat perched above the rocks at the northern end of Bondi Beach, where we played out our lustful, Ecstasy-fuelled relationship for the next eighteen months. Ecstasy, for me, meant long, dreamy, blissful afternoons in Mikhail's sundrenched bedroom. Our soundtrack was Simply Red's album, 'A New Flame', and it was only love, doing its thing—I thought. Nothing existed except our naked bodies, pleasure, the rumpled sheets, love and truth ... the sex was lazy and languid, with frequent pauses for loving exchanges.

So you can imagine how I felt one Monday morning, when I gently reminded Mikhail of something he'd suggested on the weekend—that we should move in together.

'Sahi, I was on E when I said that!'

My jaw dropped. Didn't he mean it? Why, on Ecstasy, would you say something that wasn't true? Why bother? Obviously I hadn't been listening, a few tracks later on 'A New Flame'—it seems I'd mistaken sex for something else entirely. Mikhail was urbane and sophisticated; his friends were other lawyers and academics. He would host dinner parties at his cool flat to which Orphan Annie was not invited. Orphan Annie would sulk.

It would be years before I could hear Simply Red again without feeling a momentary, residual surge of Ecstasy flood my neuroreceptors: love, truth and rumpled sheets, whispered endearments, humid Bondi afternoons.

* * *

The environmental business wasn't getting anywhere and I'd been exploring opportunities back in my comfort zone, medical sales. At Speedos Café one morning Mikhail and I had breakfast with his ex-girlfriend, Lauren, and her boyfriend, Leon. All I remember of Leon from that morning was an occasional contribution to the conversation from behind the *Sydney Morning Herald*—the Business section, if my memory serves.

Lauren knew I'd been looking for a job. She worked in medical sales too.

'Any interviews, Sahi?' she asked.

'Yep, one this Wednesday with a little company in North Ryde. Dialysis products. Very small—you won't have heard of it.'

But her eyes widened. 'What's it called?'

'Domedica.'

'Domedica!' She laughed. 'That's where I work! I'm the Product Manager in the other department, cell salvage!'

When I said Domedica was very small, I wasn't exaggerating. Each of the two 'departments' had one product manager and one sales representative, although the company did boast a small production facility where some dialysis disposables were assembled. Soon I'd secured a sales job there. And thus cemented a friendship with Lauren that I cherish to this day, with Leon too, whom Lauren soon married.

So in mid-1991 I left the flat on Parsley Bay, moved in with my old friend Elise on Bondi Road, and started work selling dialysers—artificial kidneys—at Domedica. I would soon face the reality that Mikhail and I would never be happy, but it didn't take long for Lauren and I to agree that the best thing he'd given either of us was each other.

The Domedica crew was very straight. The receptionist, production manager and accountant were all North Ryde girls, and lunchtime conversations on Mondays centred on the accountant's approaching nuptials and the other two's exploits at 'Tigers' night club on the weekend—their romantic successes or otherwise with the Balmain football players and their mates. One morning the production manager drifted blearily into work and stood pumping instant coffee granules into a polystyrene cup in the kitchen.

'How was your weekend, Linda?' I asked.

She smiled dreamily and said, 'You lower your standards and a whole new world opens up ...' Within months she was married too.

Anyway, as if living in the Eastern Suburbs wasn't seen as being alien enough, I was quickly labelled weird because I was vegetarian. When I took my first holiday and it was in India, that really got them talking (when I could have gone to *Bali*). And I'll never forget the look on the receptionist's face when I told her who I was bringing to the company Christmas party that first year—she knew Mikhail was Lauren's ex. I played innocent. Lauren and I had a lot of fun with that.

Lauren, of course, called me 'Sahi'—that's how Mikhail had introduced me to her. But in the office she had to remember to call me 'Jenny', as I was known then. My parallel existences lived on—business suits, sales targets and spreadsheets all week: sarongs, Bondi brunches and therapy groups all weekend.

Two years later I moved to Melbourne to be closer to my biggest customers. Swarna went back to Europe and opened a high-end boutique on Mykonos. Keshava moved to Byron Bay, invested in a nightclub and dabbled with the shady end of town. Some years later his body would be found in a shallow grave on a headland, after a deal gone wrong.

* * *

Sannyas was, indeed, something I hoped to belong to. It was also the ultimate rebellion: simply being in India with its inherent dangers was an act of insurgence—my stay in Amsterdam too. The risks I took were a stand against my cautious, blinds-drawn, nuclear-family existence and the common-or-garden Anglican Christianity of my past. Just moving to the culturally diverse Eastern Suburbs and sharing a house was outside the life path my mother had envisaged for me. She'd been aghast to discover, in the kitchen in Stricklandstrasse, a salad bowl she'd given me 'being used by strangers!'—you can see why there were things I kept from her.

As for Mum's reaction to my taking sannyas, I certainly got what I'd been after. I wrote from Pune, telling her what had transpired and suggesting that she address any letters to 'Marga Sahi' as otherwise they might not reach me. It wasn't true and I cringe now at my mendacity. Mum complied, but of course the letters inside were addressed to 'Dear Jennifer'. She'd given me 'a perfectly good name' and 'damned' if she would ever call me anything else. When I got back to Sydney she told me she'd found a psychiatrist who specialised in reversing 'brainwashing' and she'd like to pay for an appointment (I declined the offer). She must have been very concerned, but she slowly reconciled herself to the idea and a few years later even conceded that she thought sannyas had been good for me.

But did I belong? *Do* I belong?

At times I've felt like an outsider in the sannyas communities where I've lived. I've always maintained strong links with the non-sannyas world through work (always those parallel lives). There has always been the Jen/Sahi, professional/social divide—a distinction that has blurred more and more over recent years, as friends become clients and clients become friends. In a small, close community, it's hard to keep those groups separate. There have been times, sometimes annoying, sometimes funny, when the two names have caused confusion. When I started a relationship with one boyfriend, James, he decided that he would prefer to call me Jen. It was his call. But a mutual friend, who only knew me as Sahi, admitted to me later that at first she thought he was two-timing me. 'Sahi, he was waxing lyrical about his new love called Jen, and you'd told me *you* were seeing him,' said Lois. 'I thought, he *does* move fast!'

So, do I belong? When my partner Hansa was considering making a move on me in 2006—we'd been friends for eight years but finally we were both single at the same time—he was worried about how my MS might impact me, or us, in the future. Would he be able to meet the challenge of my care, should it come to that?

He asked his good friend Nijanando what he thought, and later he relayed Nij's answer to me. I still well up a little when I recall it.

'Hansa, if the shit hits the fan for Sahi, we're all going to be there anyway. We're family. So why don't you go for it and enjoy some good times now?'

For me, that's belonging.

4. a kind of slipstream

Did I really move to Melbourne 'to be closer to my biggest customers'? That's what I told my boss. But I had moved to Melbourne, if I'm honest, to get away from Mikhail. We had too many friends in common and it was painful to see him at parties, even to see his car on the street. I needed a new start, far away.

No, wait. I was still in love with Mikhail. I knew that it wasn't the right time for us, but that sooner or later he would realise what he'd lost, and turn up penitent at my door. I did need to get away, but just to be sure he would always be able to find me I moved to Melbourne, where he had gone to university and where his best friends still lived. I knew these friends—in fact, they were almost the only people I knew when I first arrived in Melbourne—and set about establishing independent friendships with them. This seemed to take the form of babysitting for them all, quite often ... but that's the price you pay for love.

When I wasn't required for babysitting, I immersed myself in the Melbourne music scene—sax solos and scat at smoky jazz bars like Bennetts Lane in the city, complex African rhythms at the Moomba Hotel in West Melbourne, and anything that was playing at the Rainbow Hotel in Fitzroy. I even bought a saxophone and started taking lessons. But I didn't progress much further than scales and a quavery, stilted version of *The Girl from Ipanema*, and decided that I'd rather spend my time and money supporting real musicians. I also loved Melbourne's cafés and bookshops, especially—in winter—the ones with couches and log fires.

Perhaps the strongest friendship I formed in Melbourne was with Sue Evans and her husband, Bill Thomson. I already knew Sue—I had inherited her as a customer when, still in Sydney, I was promoted to Renal Product Manager at Domedica. She ran the renal unit at one of Melbourne's major public hospitals, one of Domedica's biggest accounts and ostensibly one of the clients I'd moved to Melbourne to service better. The outgoing Product Manager had told me, 'Be really careful with Sue Evans. She can be quite intimidating, and we can't afford to lose that account!'

So it was with some trepidation that I'd arrived at her office for my first appointment.

I sat myself primly on the visitor's chair at her desk and made polite enquiries as to the health of Sue and her staff. I ascertained that all was going well with the new plasma filtration device they'd started using, and that the luer-locks on the bloodlines were no longer leaking. All had gone spiffingly, and I was ready to pick up my briefcase and leave. But Sue had other ideas.

She leaned across her desk. 'Do you have half an hour to spare?'

'Of course,' I said. Even if I didn't, I wasn't about to say no to the formidable Sue Evans.

'Good! Because you're about the same height as my husband ... I just need to check something.' She grabbed her smart handbag (Sue always wore great shoes and carried excellent bags) and I followed her out the door. Ten minutes later I found myself climbing, in my stocking feet, with Sue into an empty spa bath in a showroom down the road. Intimidating? Formidable? 'Perfect!' she said.

And thus commenced one of the least conventional customer relationships I've had. I often had dinner with Sue and Bill when I was in Melbourne. Sue and I would share hotel rooms at international conferences (you got away with that in those days, before ethical oversight—Sue was just happy to save her department's money). So when I eventually moved to Melbourne in 1993, Sue was delighted. She even used to feed my cat, Paspatu, when I travelled—and I travelled a lot. She and Bill are both amongst my closest friends to this day.

But, as close as I was to Sue, she had no idea of my other life—sannyas. I had made contact with the sannyas community in Melbourne. It was a shadow of the vibrant, busy sannyas community in Sydney but I still went to the occasional party, or did weekend therapy or meditation groups. I had thoroughly compartmentalised my two lives. It wasn't until I left Domedica and had no professional reputation to protect that I let Sue and Bill into my secret, parallel existence. At the time, they appeared to take it in their stride. It was only years later that Sue confessed to me how confused she'd been—not that I *had* this other existence, but about whether, and how, she could still play a part in my life.

'I'd thought we were good friends, but then I started to wonder where Bill and I fitted in your life—your exciting, alternative life,' she said. 'Our life was so corporate, so conventional ... what was our place in *your* life? And, by the way, what should we *call* you now?'

Sue Evans—conventional? But when she told me this, much later, I was filled with sadness. I hadn't trusted them, and that was unjustified. And it underlined for me the schizoid life I'd created, and made myself live, for so many years. No wonder I was exhausted.

***

In March 1994 I'd been in Melbourne for a year. I awoke one morning, opened my eyes, and noticed something strange.

If I looked steadily ahead everything was okay, but as soon as I moved my eyes left or right ghosts of objects started to trail in a kind of slipstream.

I caught a taxi to see my GP. 'Sudden onset double vision,' he pronounced, and sent me straight to the Melbourne Eye and Ear Hospital. After a scan ruled out a brain tumour, a specialist advised me to go home and rest. In fact there wasn't much else I could do. I certainly couldn't drive—just walking down the street was an adventure. I couldn't even read. For four weeks I lay on the sofa with the cat and listened to music until I was able to start moving around safely again.

After six weeks my vision had almost returned to normal. This was a huge relief to me; I'd booked myself into the Hoffman Process, a week-long, intensive, residential therapy program, intrigued by the sales tag-line: *It's never too late to have a happy childhood.* And I didn't want anything getting in my way.

I was twenty-eight. Despite sannyas group therapy I was still wrestling with my past, entering and ending unsatisfactory relationships with inappropriate men (Mikhail, unsurprisingly, had not shown up at my Melbourne door), or sabotaging relationships with quite appropriate ones, feeling resentful and despairing, believing that there was some point of acceptance or forgiveness that I must attain in order to become a whole person.

I'm seven years old. Daddy has my wrist and my brother's enclosed tightly in his huge hand. I can feel my bones grinding against Jon's, and it hurts.

Who's the strongest? *Daddy demands. Jon has started to cry. He's only five. He's not the strongest. I can feel myself giving in, but I try to wrench my arm away. It just hurts more.*

Who's the strongest? Eh? Who's the strongest?

I relent. You're the strongest, Daddy. *He laughs and lets go.*

I'm twenty-eight. I'm in bed with my lover. He's lying on me, holding me down with his weight, restraining me. We're both laughing and I'm enjoying the struggle.

He grabs my wrists and forces them down against the bed. I pull against him, in mock resistance at first, then I start to panic. He won't let go. I'm growling and writhing with all my strength, and he's laughing. He thinks I'm playing.

With a cry like a wild animal, I surge up and forces my knee into his groin. He lets go and rolls into a ball, gagging.

* * *

I felt that when I'd finally screamed, thrashed around and bashed enough mattresses with baseball bats, I would emerge whole, happy and ready to start my life. In the mid-nineties there was no end of therapists, self-help books and residential retreats that encouraged this belief. A happy childhood after all?

So one autumn morning I drove two hours down the Bellarine Peninsula south west of Melbourne and fronted up to a leafy, secluded conference centre. I was nervous and excited and full of anticipation.

At the front desk a smiling receptionist welcomed me with a key to my room—a room that I would hardly see, save for some disoriented minutes book-ending a few hours of shattered, dream-infested sleep each night. For the next week about twenty of us—young, middle class professionals in the main—met early for breakfast every day then convened in a big, bright room to sit in a circle of chairs with two Hoffman facilitators. Wary at first, I came to know and trust some of my Hoffman comrades like, well, family. We shared our stories—childhood sadnesses, adult catastrophes—and engaged in deep meditation, guided visualisation and group therapy until late every night.

The tissue boxes scattered around the room were replenished daily. I doubt there would have been one ten minute interval in the whole week where no-one cried. At times, ragged with exhaustion, we *laughed* until we cried. A red-headed human relations manager and I compiled a 'Catalogue of Weeping' (apologies to Leunig), inspired by our co-participants' assorted styles of sobbing, sniffling and wailing—fully attributed. We performed it one lunchtime to, I believe, unadulterated appreciation.

During one very moving guided visualisation I held my father, as a baby, in my arms and felt the pain he experienced as a child. I knew a little of his early history. His father had walked out when Dad was seven years old, returning briefly every eleven months to beat up his wife and children and to prevent my grandmother Violet from divorcing him—in those days a woman could file for divorce on the grounds of desertion, but only after her husband had been absent for a year. Violet had tried to form other relationships during those years. With pride, Dad had told us of the day, only fifteen at the time, he knocked one of these men to the ground after he—the boyfriend—had insulted Violet. Then Dad left home and joined the merchant navy.

I felt, that day of 'the Process', I had come to an understanding of the root of Dad's damage, and thus his behaviour as a parent, and could absolve him of blame. I felt a real sense of forgiveness, and it felt good.

But at the end of the course, believing myself to be on the way to healing, I was somewhat disconcerted to learn the final assignment.

'You need to tell both your parents that you love them,' said the course instructor.

I blanched. I could probably manage to tell Mum, although the L-word had never been a part of our family's vernacular. But Dad?

'Um, that won't be possible,' I explained to the instructor. 'You see, I don't talk to my father. Haven't for years.' I hadn't even laid eyes on him since moving out of home eight years before.

The instructor smiled sadly, shaking his head. 'Sorry, no excuses.'

And maybe because I still thought I could be healed, maybe because I'd paid thousands of dollars for this program and was determined to wring every last cent of value out of it, I decided that I would do it. The following week I flew to Sydney.

Part Two

1. how to be liked

My parents met on the Dutch liner *Willem Ruys* on its way from London to Sydney in 1962. Dad was an Aussie crew member (he'd gone to sea at fifteen), and Mum was emigrating with her parents and brother, 'Ten Pound Poms'. Her sister had already married an Australian and settled here.

It sounds very romantic, doesn't it? Boy meets girl on ocean liner ... with a uniform thrown in. The way Mum told it, Dad was trying to solve an algebra problem for his Second Mate's Certificate one evening, and she, ever the school teacher, was helping him with it. That was it. Mum felt clever and useful, and Dad liked her legs.

I see them there—Dad, bearded, lean and tanned in his khakis, Mum, shy and pretty—huddled over a page of scribbled equations in the third class dining room, their heads close, murmuring ... the scrape of cutlery on china as the galley staff clear plates around them, the thrum of the engine and the steady heave of the Indian Ocean below, my grandmother pausing in the doorway to look back, her brow furrowed. And I want to grab them by the shoulders and shake them. *Don't do it! You'll be miserable! Please, just walk away ...*

But Mum was twenty-five, Dad twenty-nine, both too old to be single in the early 1960s. They wrote to each other while Mum got teaching work in Sydney and Dad continued to crew ships. He sent her a pearl necklace—Mikimoto—from Japan. They married in December 1963. Dad 'went ashore', trying various lines of work including real estate sales and taxi driving.

The newlyweds decided on Sydney's northern suburbs and Dad, being in the business, kept a close eye on listings. They bought a Federation bungalow in Violet Street, Balgowlah, a fixer-upper, and fixed it up. I was born in 1965, the perfect Dr Spock baby, or so my mother said—I was sleeping through the night at six weeks.

Jonathan, born two years after me, wasn't the perfect Dr Spock baby. Mum's pregnancy had been difficult. I suspect that by then things weren't so rosy between her and Dad. Dad was drinking a lot—maybe he was finding it hard to adjust to shore life after nineteen years at sea. Mum had caught influenza during her first trimester; Jon was born with cataracts and was blind in his right eye. He was also prone to screaming at night. Mum gave him Valium so we could all get some sleep.

Jon and I got off to a bad start. For two years I'd been an only child used to unlimited attention and privileges, and here, suddenly, was this red-faced, squalling creature commanding all of Mum's emotional resources. I hated it when Mum paid him attention. I wouldn't leave her alone so she had to shut herself away with him. An early memory: I'm jumping up at a door handle, and screaming. Mum's behind that door with Jon. I'm crying, trembling with indignation, then I can smell hot pee and my legs are wet.

I have no idea how Mum managed when Dad gave up and went back to sea. One day I sat in the bay window of the front room, watching through the leadlight panes as Dad swung a blue carry bag into a taxi on the street below. Mum was standing beside me, holding tiny Jon, and both were crying.

'I don't *like* you, Jennifer,' Mum would say. It became a refrain. Or, 'I'm ashamed of you.' Another was, 'We were having *such* a lovely day and now you've *spoilt* it'. Oh, the guilty sting of that one, not just that the day was no longer lovely, but that all the lovely things that had happened that day were suddenly as nothing, due to some cruel or selfish or thoughtless act of mine. The shame of it was a hot, hard little knot in my gut. But I couldn't help it. She was right. I didn't like me either.

Many years later, Dad admitted to me that he'd never wanted children. I suppose, in the sixties, such preferences weren't discussed between marrying couples. I'm not surprised that he soon went back to sea. And imagine Mum, being left to deal with a fractious newborn and a resentful two-year-old, alone. It's true that her parents lived nearby and were very supportive, but this caused a whole other set of problems because Dad had never got on with Mum's father. Mum told me that when I was born Dad was working at the paper factory Poppa managed in Brookvale. Mum had been in labour for almost two days when the hospital called to say that my arrival was imminent. Poppa told Dad to finish what he was doing before leaving, then he, Poppa, got in his car and drove to the hospital himself. He was the first one there, the first one to see me.

***

My first address, 7 Violet Street. I feel I should be writing it in carefully pencilled letters on the back of an envelope. A child's return address.

We did return to Violet Street once, Dad and I. It was in 1996, during those strange years in my late twenties, early thirties, after the Hoffman Process. We were trying, or I think he was trying and I know I was, to establish a father-daughter relationship. I would use the word 'reconcile' here except that it implies the recapturing of a former way of being. But Dad and I were in new territory.

I suspect that Dad had always wanted to go back to Violet Street—out of nosiness rather than any sense of nostalgia. And he had me with him that day, in 1996, so he'd be more comfortable knocking on the current residents' front door and asking if he could poke around. When we were kids and there was a house for sale in the neighbourhood, and he wanted to have a look—not to buy, just out of interest—he'd take a couple of us kids so that, he told Mum, no-one would think he was there to case the joint.

The day Dad and I went to Violet Street we went up the side of the house. Dad squatted down beside a downpipe at the back corner and pointed at three tiny pairs of footprints set in the concrete, labelled 'Jennifer', 'Jonathan' and 'Matthew', with dates written beneath.

The big, concrete-edged sandpit Dad had built for us, where we used to dig up cat droppings and present them to Mum in a bucket, was still there, but now it was a garden bed. So was the sprawling willow tree, but gone was the car tyre Dad had hung on the end of a rope from a branch. I once nearly choked on a purple Lifesaver I was sucking while hanging upside down on that swing, and when it dislodged, at last, in one final, racking spew, I thought I'd spat a gob of blood into my hand.

We didn't go inside. I would have loved to but it felt a bit intrusive. Even being in the garden felt a bit strange, but being with Dad always felt a bit strange, even when he was sober. We thanked the woman and told her about the footprints, then we left.

***

Returning to early '68, when Dad went back to sea. Thus began the rhythm of our family life. Dad sailed on the MV *Macedon*, a medium-sized bulk carrier transporting potash from Adelaide to Sydney. When I was eight Mum learnt to drive and we would go to pick Dad up from the ship when it docked at Pyrmont. Jonathan and I would tear around the decks, peer into the huge cargo holds full of fine, white powder, clamber down long, steep ladders to marvel at the clanging, smelly engine room, and hang off the giant, polished timber wheel in the bridge before being treated to fizzy drinks in the smoky 'mess' with its felt-lined, lipped tabletops. I doubt such free-ranging would be allowed these days. Maybe it wasn't then, but by that time we were the First Mate's kids, so the crew would have turned a blind eye.

Dad would do three return trips to Adelaide, then take six weeks' leave while the other crew did three trips. But even while he was 'at sea', he'd be home for thirty-six hours each time the ship tied up at Pyrmont to unload the cargo. So Dad was a stranger to us for six weeks of every twelve, dropping in for a day and a half every ten days to turn our lives upside down. Even when on leave, he was uninterested in us and easily irritated. We got used to hearing 'Buzz off!' We knew what that meant: it was time to make ourselves scarce. It meant he could turn nasty, and quickly. We'd flap our arms, making buzzing noises, and run away. But there was no comedy in our rapid departure.

***

I have a photo. There's a date pencilled on the back in Mum's small, neat hand: May '71. We're sitting on wide, stone steps in a formal garden: Dad, Jon and I. There's lawn and a big, circular flower garden in the distance. And a tumble of some white-flowered ground cover spilling onto the steps beside us.

Dad's wearing a cardigan. He's in stove-pipe trousers which have ridden up a little to show some pale shin,

dark socks and leather slip-on shoes, a pale buttoned shirt. I'm in a woollen jumper and plaid skirt, white knee-high socks and white patent-leather shoes with a strap and buckle. There's a big white bow in my shoulder-length hair, which Mum has let me start to grow now I'm at school. Jon's wearing dark cord trousers and a woollen jumper. We always had woollen jumpers, hand-knitted by Mum or Nana.

Dad sits on the top step, hands clasped loosely between his knees. Jon and I mimic his posture, unconsciously. Or not. I sit beside Dad, Jon between his feet on the step below.

Mum would have been behind the camera, off to the side. We couldn't have known she was taking a photo: we're not looking at her, but at something straight ahead of us. Or, Jon and I are. Dad's looking down, maybe at Jon, but really almost *through* him. Like he'd be looking at the ground between his feet, were Jon not there. His brow is lined and his mouth tight.

It's unusual to see a photo of us not looking at the camera. Mum would always be there, eyebrows raised in excitement, the camera at her face, shutter-finger poised. 'Smile, everyone ... please smile, Brian ...'

Gazing at this photo now, forty five years later, another scene comes to me, unbidden. It's a little later that day and we've had ice-creams, Mr Whippy cones. I can hear the piped notes of *Greensleeves* fading into the distance and my lips are sweet and sticky. Jon has dripped his ice-cream down his jumper and Mum is swiping at it, and at his face, with a spit-moistened hankie. He's wailing. Dad has left—in frustration? Disgust? Just a wish to be away from this woman, these children, this fussing? He's halfway back to the car, and Jon's on tiptoes, peering over Mum's shoulder, following him with his eyes. He thinks we're losing him.

Is this a memory? Or just a reverie? Of all of us, Jon always had the best distance vision.

* * *

Dad went to visit Mr Sinclair on the corner one day and took Jon and me with him.

'Would you kids like a soft drink?' asked the kindly old man.

Jon and I looked at each other. 'What's a soft drink?' I asked.

'A *fizzy drink!* A soft drink is a *fizzy drink,*' Dad sneered. Then he turned to Mr Sinclair and laughed. 'Their mother's a Pom,' he said. 'They pick up all kinds of funny stuff.'

Mr Sinclair pulled two cold, bright green Schweppes bottles out of the fridge and poked a straw into each. I sipped on mine and puzzled over where I'd gone wrong. Dad had laughed but I knew that I'd embarrassed him. I felt ashamed to have let him down.

In our Violet Street bedroom I would lie awake at night, listening to Jonathan breathing in the other bed. He would take a deep breath, close his throat with a click, hold it for a while, then release it in a rush. Each time, I would wait in the silence, holding my own breath until he breathed out.

* * *

From the age of five I was prone to sore throats and ear aches. I always seemed to have eardrop-dampened cotton balls stuffed in my ears and crushed white pills in sticky red cordial to swallow off a teaspoon. Mum asked our family doctor if there might be a case for having my tonsils removed, but he didn't think surgery was necessary. He assured her that the infections would stop by the time I was eleven—in the meantime the antibiotics would keep them at bay. He was eventually proven right but in the meantime I'd had three or four courses of penicillin per year for six years.

At school I was a high-achiever—academically. Socially I was isolated and confused. I always felt different. Even my lunches were weird: all the other kids' sandwiches were peanut butter or vegemite; mine were sardines or liverwurst. They brought apples for afterwards; I brought tomatoes.

Mrs van der Linde is the music teacher at infants' school. She's not like the other teachers. She's tall and tanned, and wears long, flowing clothes with bare legs and flat leather sandals. The other teachers wear pantyhose and closed shoes with little heels. Mrs van der Linde's hair is wavy and loose to her shoulders; the other teachers have neat buns or short, prim hairstyles. Mrs van der Linde's feet are long and brown and her second toe on each foot is longer than her big toe.

I know about Mrs van der Linde's toes because at music time the children all sit cross-legged on the floor at the front of the classroom, and she hands out instruments that we strike or shake or rattle while she strums her guitar, singing and tapping her long, brown feet.

Today, as usual, we all hold our breath waiting to see who will get The Drum. Mrs van der Linde hands out the boring triangles and castanets and maracas, then picks up The Drum and turns to Tony Strong.

'Tony, today you can play the drum,' she says, smiling brightly.

Tony's one of the class Bad Boys. This morning, Tony had to call his mother to confess to some badness or another. I had been walking past the headmistress's office that morning, probably on some errand (I'm often sent on errands, being a good, clever girl) and had seen Tony standing behind Mrs Webb's desk, holding the black telephone receiver to his ear with both hands. Tony has a shock of yellow hair, a crooked grin and a gravelly voice. He'd winked at me as I peered in.

'Tony had to ring his mother,' I tell Mrs van der Linde. Well, someone had to tell her, before it was too late. I imagine the look of gratitude Mrs van der Linde will bestow upon me. I've saved her, just in time, from a huge mistake: rewarding Tony, who had to call his mother that very day, with The Drum.

Mrs van der Linde's smile fades and her face turns dark, as I expected. But she casts her eyes about and her black gaze lands on ... me.

'And what does that have to do with anything?'

I look down and pick at my shoelaces. I knew he was ringing his mother. To my mind, there could be no worse punishment. I'd rather die than have to admit any misdemeanour to my own mother. In our house, goodness is the most important thing in the world, even more important than being able to spell long words.

But Tony Strong's bad and he's allowed to play The Drum too. And instead of thanking me for my helpfulness, Mrs van der Linde is angry with me.

She gives me one last dirty look, hands the drumsticks to Tony Strong, and begins to strum.

I just didn't know how to be likeable. I didn't know how to be *liked*. One day in Year Three I crept up behind two little girls sitting together on a bench in the playground—maybe sharing their lunch, or a book, or something else that normal little girls enjoyed—and knocked their heads together. *Clunk.* It had been funny when Moe did it to Larry and Curly on TV. But the little girls both burst out crying and

I was sent to the principal for a stern lecture about consideration and kindness.

It was about then that I developed a cough—just a mild, unobtrusive little *ahem*. At the time there was no apparent infection. After a few months, with no more symptoms, it was deemed to be a 'nervous cough', which was apparently preferable to the infectious kind. I also started punctuating my speech with a little chuckle, *heh-heh*, after every utterance. I was awkward and embarrassed about, well, everything. I tried to copy other little girls—I read all the horse books I could find because Jeanette Hoogstad and Samantha Edwards went horse-riding at the weekend. I hunched over the kitchen radio to write lists of songs and artists because the other girls knew the names of pop singers. I practised walking pigeon-toed because it was so fetching when Samantha did it. I nagged Mum to buy Vegemite.

I realise now how many times I made friends with 'the new girl' at school. Every year, if a new girl arrived in my class, I assigned myself as her caretaker. It began in Year One with Leanne, a German girl who buried her face in her mother's belly at the door of our classroom the day she started. In Year Three Prue arrived from New Zealand. Louise, from Melbourne, turned up in Year Four. In Year Eight Urte, also from Germany, arrived. Elizabeth from Wellington (in country NSW) in Year Nine. Tracey in

Year Eleven. All of them I took under my wing—until they found their feet and were absorbed into the general, happy throng of my classmates.

Maybe I was thinking, deep down, that here was someone who didn't know (yet) how unlikeable I was. Here was a chance to be liked. A fresh start.

I did have one close friend, Elise. I can't remember how we really met, because classes were divided up alphabetically by surname and we were never in the same one. Nor can I remember us ever playing together at school, but from infants' school we visited each other's houses after school and on weekends. More often I would go to hers. Later we went to the same high school. She was a rock in my life, knew what was going on at home (I was otherwise quite private about my troubles) and in Year Ten, when I had to find somewhere else to live for a while, it would be to Elise's house I fled.

At home in Violet Street I had two friends: Cathy next door and Simone across the road. They were Catholic girls and a source of wonder for me—on Sundays I caught rare glimpses of them at best, in pretty dresses and shoes, their hair brushed and pinned, on their way to Mass or some other mysterious destination with their families. But on Saturdays we used to sneak into St Cecilia's church down the hill, light all the votive candles, drip wax everywhere, then run away. We begged left-over balls of wool from our mothers and twisted lengths into rainbow-hued 'bookmarks', which we hawked up and down Violet Street for two cents (or five cents for the long ones), then solemnly presented our earnings to old Miss Ewatt in No. 26, who collected for The House With No Steps. We held meetings of the Chatterbox Club in Cathy's Dad's garden shed—hushed, top-secret affairs which we often had to abandon abruptly, shrieking and pinching our noses, when our brothers shoved handfuls of squashed and reeking citrus beetles, collected from the lemon tree, under the locked door. We had to be still and quiet when Mrs Lumsdaine in No. 11 let us sit in her lounge room to play 'Explosive Hits '74' (at low volume) on her record player—my treasured first record, a hand-me-down from my cousin, Caron. I would sniffle through *Billy, Don't be a Hero* and *Seasons in the Sun*, my hankie jammed in my mouth. But we couldn't sit still to *Devil Gate Drive* or *The Loco-motion*. We'd wriggle and bop silently on the sofa.

* * *

Three things happened in rapid succession the year I turned ten.

Firstly, Dad quit smoking. He'd developed a hacking cough and an x-ray showed a suspicious shadow on his lung. It turned out to be pneumonia but it must have scared him. He was only forty-two. He gave up the cigarettes and cigars he'd smoked for twenty-five years.

Next, my maternal grandmother died, quite suddenly, of a heart attack.

I get home from school and the front door's open. There are voices in the lounge room. Mummy, Daddy, Auntie Julie, Uncle Arthur and Auntie Karen are all there, and my cousins, Caron and Peter. I know that something's up—Auntie Karen has her feet, in strappy, buckled sandals, up beside her on the couch and Mummy's not saying anything about it.

Mummy takes me by the shoulder and steers me into her bedroom. Her eyes are red and swollen. I can't remember what she says but I'm thinking about when Nana and Poppa went on holiday and Poppa brought me back a postcard of the aeroplane they went on, with clouds and sky behind. But this time Nana's never coming back.

Mummy rings Louise's mum and asks if I can spend the night at their house, and packs me a bag, and soon I'm in Louise's dad's car, leaving Mummy and everyone behind. I cry all night and the next day at school. Louise has to tell the teacher why.

Nana was short and plump and cuddly, and loved to bake. Her kitchen smelled of yeast and cinnamon and she had a permanent dusting of icing sugar on her pillowy bosom. She taught me how to cross-stitch with coloured threads on scraps of cloth, and we poked geranium cuttings into the moist, warm soil of her flower beds and watched them grow and flower. We mixed scone dough in her sunny kitchen and gently folded it, over and over, then rolled it, cut perfect rounds with a floured glass and watched them through the glass on her oven door as they rose and turned golden. She tucked me into her soft spare bed on the nights I was lucky enough to spend at her house, and heaped on the blankets and quilts. I burrowed under the weight of the covers and felt warm and safe and loved.

Nana could always be depended upon for a cuddle. Mum didn't hold or hug us and even when we were babies her physical contact with us was limited to the bare necessities. She said later that Dad had warned her we'd end up homosexual if she touched us too much; I suppose that worried her.

So Dad stopped smoking, Nana died, then, within weeks of Nana's death, we left the neat blocks and footpaths of Balgowlah for the sweeping, shady gardens of harbour side Seaforth—a neighbouring suburb. It may have been a step up in socio-economic status but it heralded, for me, a slide into ten years of pain, fear and confusion.

2. a balancing act

We moved to 2 Sangrado Street in December 1975. Seaforth descended gently from the Sydney Road shopping strip to the lush water frontages, and Sangrado Street was a short cul-de-sac right on Middle Harbour. At its end was a steep flight of steps which led down to Powderhulk Bay, with its shabby sailing club and swimming baths, and glittering waters studded with small yachts bobbing on buoys. Sangrado Street and the steps formed one boundary of a triangular patch of remnant bushland. A private road ran down one other side, and the muddy sands and oyster-encrusted rocks of the bay formed the third. But between these was a wilderness—at least to kids used to the suburban cross-streets and nature-strips of Balgowlah: a few acres surrounding a stormwater run-off we called 'The Creek'. With its waterfalls and wooden bridges it was a cool and shady retreat in summer, and the domain of endless treasure hunts and games of hide-and-seek, chasings and bush-skill-acquiring activities.

Within days of our moving, the summer holidays began and we joined the gang of kids who gathered on a grassy patch across the road every morning for French cricket or tip footy. There were the two Scotts, the Flack kids—although they were a bit younger—and Richard who was much older and bigger but who deigned to attend anyway. One day playing tip footy he dislocated Scott B's shoulder in a tackle and we had to race down the street on our dragsters and summon Scott's mum, who arrived in the family car and whisked him away to Manly Hospital.

Some of the boys had skateboards and we all had wheels of some sort, except our little brother Matthew who was only three. Matthew got separated from us one day and eventually came home with ten cents in his pocket. After some intense questioning Mum had some warnings for the other mothers about a quiet teenage boy, not in our gang, who lived on Aden Street.

When we overheated on hot afternoons, we all ran home for our swimmers and towels and met at the harbour baths at the bottom of that long flight of steps. There was a diving platform at the back, with a long, rattan-covered board where we'd line up to do 'bombs' into the water. Then we'd clamber back up the ladder, careful to avoid the oyster shells waiting to slice our feet around its lower rungs.

One summer afternoon when I was eleven I cut my foot badly while climbing the ladder and dripped blood all the way up the steps. Once home, I showered, washed and dressed the wound, then revelled in the empty house. The whole family, even Mum, was down at the pool—a rare occasion. I put on a soft, yellow, cotton jumpsuit from the hippie shop in Manly and my favourite album, America's 'History: Greatest Hits'. The scar, still visible, brings back to me the music, that warm, balmy evening, drifting from room to empty room, feeling self-reliant, sensual and feminine. It may have been my first happy experience of aloneness.

Oysters also clustered on the rocks at the shallow end of the pool, so the only safe way in or out was a balancing act from pylon to pylon along the salty timber sleepers that topped the barnacle-encrusted iron bars.

It's early morning. I'm out on the diving platform with my fishing basket, dangling a line, when I notice a tall, lean man making his way out along the sleepers. He's wearing loose white shorts and a white T-shirt. He smiles and sits down beside me. I smile back—a bit.

'Hello, I'm Jim,' *he says.*

'Hello,' *I mumble.*

'Caught anything?'

I show him my bucket. Two poisonous toadies I can't even give to the cats.

'Do you know Dianne and Vicki?' *he asks.*

I think about it. There aren't many girls around here at all, or maybe they just stay inside. 'No ...'

'They're about your age. We sometimes play Doctors and Nurses. Would you like to play with us one day?'

I grip my fishing rod a bit tighter. For a start, I'm indignant. I'm much too old for Doctors and Nurses. But something else is wrong. I look down and notice that a long, brown thing is poking out of his shorts leg. It makes me feel a bit scared and a bit grown-up at the same time.

Be polite to grown-ups, Mum has always said. But don't talk to strangers, too. 'No, thanks,' *I say, reeling in my line.* 'That sounds nice but I don't think so. But thanks very much.' *I pick up my basket and bucket and start back. That line of sleepers has never felt so long. When I get to the rocks I look back; Jim*

Long Road to Dry River

is still sitting on the diving platform, gazing out at the harbour. Still, I run all the way home.

Scott B was closest in age to Jon and me and was our chief playmate in the bush. In the summer of '77 he and his family went on a long holiday. We looked after Scott's Border collie, Doggles, collected their mail and watered their garden. But we also spent much of that time devising an intricate treasure hunt with clues secreted throughout the bush and a magnificent reward at the end, the exact nature of which escapes me now. We anticipated presenting the opening clue to Scott upon his return.

But by the time Scott's family came home, Scott had turned thirteen. He looked the same but was different in a way that we couldn't quite define. The treasure remained unhunted. The next summer storm turned the creek into a temporary deluge, and the clues were all washed out to sea.

***

The Seaforth Scout Hall was across the road, at the foot of the grassy block we played cricket on. I joined the Girl Guides at twelve, learned the words to *Ging Gang Gooli* and achieved a couple of badges—I remember some tiny, soggy pancakes cooked on an upturned tin can over a candle—but *A Country*

Practice aired on Tuesday and Wednesday nights and the anguish of missing the second hour every week soon won out.

* * *

Even the garden at No. 2 was prime ground for adventures. Our block was the only one in Sangrado Street that hadn't been subdivided, due to the easement running under it (the stormwater drain that fed 'The Creek'). So the front garden was huge, with a sweeping driveway, lofty liquid ambers, willows and gums—all great climbing and cicada-collecting trees—and rock-garden borders down both sides. Mum descended on it with her trowels and forks that first summer, and proceeded to unearth all manner of mysterious artefacts, mostly medical in nature—rusted tubes of ointments and small, amber glass phials, labels and stoppers long gone. We knew that a doctor's family had lived there previously. Of more interest was an x-ray film Mum dug out of a tangled bed on the western fence. We rinsed it off and propped it up against the kitchen window for a few days, cross-referencing the blurry image with the illustrative plates in Mum's college text *Pathological Conditions in Early Childhood*—the only vaguely medical book in the house—but couldn't even identify the body part, let alone the disease.

Long Road to Dry River

* * *

Prospective paedophiles aside, Sangrado Street was a daytime paradise for me and my brothers. But as the evenings descended, the neighbourhood mothers could be heard shrieking from front porches for their broods to come in to dinner. And night-time inside No. 2 could be dark and foreboding.

Soon after that move to Seaforth, Mum decided that she was sick of serving two dinners: an early sitting for the children and a later one for her and Dad. During the first school term of 1976 she started taking casual teaching work (she had not taught since I was born) and this probably contributed to her decision. So now we all sat at the one table. This was the only regular meeting of the whole family, and it had never happened before, so maybe it's why I suddenly became aware of the terse conversations, the muttered grievances. Or maybe it was Dad's nicotine withdrawal, or that he didn't like Mum working—whatever it was, it was here to stay. When Dad was home, every night I retreated to my room after dinner with a stomach ache.

Mum, Dad and Poppa are sitting at the dining table. My brothers and I have eaten and excused ourselves.

Poppa has been living with us since Nana died two months ago. He's talking louder and louder, and Dad's answering through gritted teeth. I stand just inside my darkened bedroom doorway, heart thudding. I can't not watch.

'Go on, hit me,' Poppa says to Dad. He takes off his glasses, folds them and places them on the table. He raises his chin. 'Go on, then,' he says. He's smiling.

Dad rises from his chair.

Mum is crying. 'He wants you to do it, Brian!'

Dad sits back down and Poppa gets up, picks up his glasses and leaves the table, still grinning at Dad.

The next day Poppa's gone.

Around this time Jonathan began to hum—loudly, tunelessly, and seemingly unconsciously—at mealtimes. It went unremarked.

* * *

When Mum went back to work, she had her own money for the first time.

When I get home from school one day, Mum brings a David Jones bag into my room. She pulls out a pretty bedspread. Together we pull my musty, drab, green quilt off the bed and arrange the new cover. It's white with little orange posies and drops all the way to the floor all around. It has a matching pillowcase with a frilled border.

Mum's sitting on the end of the bed, smiling and drinking coffee. I know just what a little girl should do at that moment—I've seen Cindy do it on The Brady Bunch*—I jump on Mum's lap and give her a hug. The coffee spills on the new bedspread. Mum jumps up—'Jennifer! For goodness' sake!'—and drags the bedspread off the bed and out to the laundry.*

Those coffee stains fade over the years but never entirely disappear.

I was still trying to find my way, working out how to be a normal girl. Undeterred, I tried again that Christmas.

Uncle Arthur gives me a small parcel and I remove layers of tissue paper to reveal a fragile ceramic horse. It has 'Beswick' on its belly. Auntie Karen knows about these things and says it's special. I think, what do little girls do? I smile and widen my eyes and chatter on about how beautiful it is, and that I now have a set of three and how important that is (I'm making this up as I go). Uncle Arthur goes very quiet, then gives me a hug. He looks sad.

* * *

I've always been a writer, almost as long as I've been a reader. And I began to read before I started school. I learned to read upside down, because Mum sat opposite me or by the side of my bed to read me stories, and she realised too late that I was following the text. I had a ferocious argument with Mrs MacDonald in kindergarten—I was adamant that the first letter of my name was traced like an f, but without the crossbar. She won, but I can still read upside down almost as fast as the conventional way.

So I quickly learned the right way to orientate text and started amassing a collection of Golden Books. I read for fun, I read to learn, but perhaps, most of all, I read to escape.

I graduated from Golden Books to Enid Blyton and read through her entire catalogue—Noddy, The Famous Five, The Secret Seven … When we moved to Seaforth we joined the local library. We visited every Friday afternoon while Mum did her shopping; I would choose my quota of five books and two magazines, line up to get them stamped by the two grim, grey ladies at the front desk then race home and devour the lot, more often than not before school on Monday morning. We were only allowed to browse the children's section so I often chose books on the basis of thickness rather than subject. And the smaller the print, the longer the read …

My parents weren't readers. Dad read *The Sun*, the tabloid afternoon Sydney newspaper. Mum might have read if she'd had time. There was a small bookcase in the lounge room with a shelf of Funk & Wagnalls, a row of sober-spined *Reader's Digest Condensed* anthologies and a handful of Arthur Hailey and Alistair MacLean novels. More interesting were *Mandingo, Drum* and *Falconhurst Fancy* by Kyle Onstott and Lance Horner, soft-porn sagas set on a fictional cotton plantation in 1830s Alabama. The plots centred on sado-masochistic sexual conquests between the white masters and mistresses and the black slaves, slave-breeding programs, 'whuppings', 'bucks' and 'bed wenches'.

The illicit thrill of discovering these paperbacks … I read late into the night, wide-eyed and flushed in the yellow pool of light cast by my bedside lamp; it was the foundation of my sex education. The books must have belonged to Dad, because Mum knew I was reading them and would have confiscated them had she been familiar with their themes.

I entered the MS Readathon each year in high school, preparing an extensive reading list (no, the

Mandingo series did not feature) and signing up sponsors. The Readathon posters sported photos of cripples on crutches, sufferers smiling wanly from wheelchairs. I don't remember being moved by their plight as much as the thrill of being allowed—no, encouraged!—to spend, for those few blissful weeks, all my free hours reading.

I filled exercise books with stories and poems. I reviewed the books I read. I kept lists of words I liked. On the front page of my *Roget's Thesaurus*, a tenth birthday gift from my Auntie Julie, I wrote and signed a statement vowing to never again use the word 'said', and listed dozens of colourful alternatives: exclaimed, shouted, murmured … ejaculated … Later in life I have reconciled with 'said', but that well-thumbed 1972 edition is still always on my desk.

A particularly vicious English mistress all but crushed my enthusiasm for writing in high school. Mrs A was stout and middle-aged, the vestiges of her prettiness crimped with bitterness. She used to clump between classes, lips a thin, pinked line, tilted at the ground, books clasped to her heavily upholstered chest.

Disappointed with the world in general, Mrs A seemed to take a particular dislike to me from Year Seven, when she signed me up to the choir, the recorder group, the netball team and the debating team, in which I mumbled my ill-formed arguments, catatonic, every Friday night. I was on a full scholarship and apparently the scholarship girl 'owed it to the school' to forego lunchtimes and more. I was always in the top stream so I had her as my English teacher every year except Year Eight, when I relished my classes and attained high marks. All my other years were confusing. I felt that I understood the subject and could do the work easily, but Mrs A consistently marked me down and criticised my work in class. I approached each new school year with dread and ended each one just a little less in love with the English language, books and reading.

My writing during those years was limited to school assignments and a series of earnest, angst-ridden poems addressed to my boyfriend, composed almost entirely of rhetorical questions (*Who am I to you? Why must I always compete for your attention?*), all consigned to the backyard incinerator almost before the ink was dry.

Then there was this poem, deemed suitable for the school magazine when I was in Year Ten.

Girls in Pink

A child is born. A girl
Attired in pink. She sleeps
With wee fists clenched; a vain attempt
To redeem her individuality.

> Months pass by. Her girlishness
> Adorned in frills and bows
> Is infused on her ungendered spirit, 'til,
> Ensnared by chains of lace
> And fetters of plastic beads
> She succumbs
> And becomes
> Woman.
>
> Years pass by; she learns of Life and Logic and Law,
> Churchill, Chamberlain
> Landform, logarithms, et s'il vous plaît?
> Until, degreed-down with the burden of PhDs
> She steps into the world of men ...
>
> Where, bedroomed and kitchened,
> She rears her produce with maternal sincerity,
> The girls in pink, with frills and beads ...
>
> While bottom-drawered degrees dustily confirm her human-hood
> To a yellowing thesis and a moth-eaten tassel.

I'm sure I meant progeny, not produce.

One weekend in Year Twelve, over tumblers of Lindeman's cask Riesling, Elise and I concocted a fantasy. Elise had a 1959 Volkswagen and we dreamt of preparing Molotov cocktails and doing a drive-by bombing of Mrs A's house in Mosman. We knew her address—although we only had a vague idea of what a Molotov cocktail was. Our classmates were aware of this. I suppose that similar talk, if it became public these days, would attract the attention of ASIO.

I didn't read a book for pleasure for another five years. Then, walking down Mahatma Gandhi Road in Pune one day, I found a tiny bookshop with a spinner of dusty, locally published international paperbacks, all at bargain prices. I snapped up a copy of *Oscar and Lucinda* by Peter Carey for about three Aussie dollars, and once again I was lost to reading—to the detriment of my meditation program.

Fast-forward to 2016. I was listening to *Life Matters* on Radio National and the presenter was asking people to call in with stories about school teachers who'd inspired them, perhaps set them on a certain life path. I found myself thinking about Mrs A. She may have changed the direction of my life, although I'm pretty sure that's not what the presenter meant.

A student in the year behind me at Redlands has since forged a successful career as a literary writer and academic in creative writing. I wondered about D. She would have been in the top stream. She would have had Mrs A year after year, and clearly it didn't put her off literature. Then again, I imagined, D might have enjoyed Mrs A's favour.

I thought, *I'm going to drop her a line.*

I found her page on the university web site and sent an email, recounting a few of my experiences and asking about hers. 'Clearly,' I said, 'she didn't put you off further studies in literature, or being a writer'. I heard nothing for ten days, and thought, *well, that's it, she was the teacher's pet*. I imagined her thinking, 'Who's this bitter, twisted person? No wonder dear Mrs A didn't have time for her.'

Then I received a reply.

D shared some stories from her years at Redlands. She'd had much the same experience of Mrs A as I—the vindictiveness, the spite, the personal vendetta. '… some part of myself—a spirit of intellectual inquiry, of writing for the sake of writing—was crushed, most particularly by Mrs A', she told me. As for her going on to study English Literature at a tertiary level, 'I do think for a very long time after leaving school there was an unhealthy "revenge" aspect to many of my achievements'. I do like the thought of an ageing Mrs A following the career of this writer whose spirit she'd tried to destroy.

D asked me how we'd coped with Mrs A's treatment, in our year. I was able to share with her a couple of moments.

First—we were required to have our end-of-year revue vetted by a senior teacher before the performance. We'd had a lot of trouble with the Mrs A skit; all the others were tinged with affection but we couldn't find it in us to bring any warmth to this one. Our geography mistress, Mrs Boyd, watched it, turned to us writers and said, 'You know, the most devastating thing you could do is just leave it out. Don't mention her at all.'

Perfect. We dropped the skit from the program.

And the class of '83 rented a beach-house at Terrigal, on the NSW Central Coast, for a couple of weeks at the end of our exams. I got up there late as 3-Unit Latin was the last exam that year, but they waited for me and we threw all our English essays, 'The A— Papers', with their red-pen scratchings, on a bonfire that night, whooping and hollering and dancing around. There may have been alcohol involved.

***

Writing this now, I feel a pang of regret that I lost touch with most of my high school friends. I feel the loss of people who knew me in those years, who might remember that awkward, insecure, socially-challenged adolescent, and who, in the end, accepted me anyway. I attended a twenty-year reunion of our class in 2003, but it had been too long. I wrote this in my head the next day, as I drove home from Sydney; if you're a child of the eighties you'll get the musical references.

> To the Class of '83
> It's the morning after our reunion and my mind swims with flashbacks and feelings I search to identify. Surging south with the traffic I emerge from the harbour tunnel. The ute finds the Eastern Distributor and the

auto-tracker finds Classic Hits Radio, and wouldn't you know it?—it's Ron E. Sparx to steer me from Sydney with the Dooby Brothers, Sting and Rod Stewart, the soundtrack of our anguished adolescence.

Who did we want to be when we were eighteen? Does anyone remember? We looked behind to the tail-end of the baby-boomers and ahead to the pioneers of an as yet unnamed Generation-x, and tried to find a footing in between.

Now I'm leaving the car yards and trade shopfronts of Sylvania behind, and rolling down into the National Park, and every breath I take has me back there.

My school years were painful. I think many of you suspected, and some of you knew, the warzone that was my family life in those years. Every afternoon I would creep stealthily back into the hostilities. Love *was* a battlefield, and now Pat Benatar hurtles with me down and around the bends of the Bulli Pass.

Thank you, Caroline, for remembering the ritual bonfire at our post-exam coastal retreat (could it have been Montego Bay?) and our sacrifice of the A— Papers. I wish I could say I was cleansed of her malevolence then and there. But the memories of her cold stare, her voice trembling with rage, the way the chalk used to snap and fly across the classroom under the fury of her grip, make my chest tighten as it did so many years ago. I heard that Mrs A also snapped, brittle as chalk, the following year and a generation of students were spared her viciousness.

Gentler memories surface. Melinda, borrowing my diary and at the end of that maths class returning it, with each religious occasion and public holiday illustrated with your quirky humour. I still think 'Yum, kippers' whenever the Jewish Day of Atonement rolls around. Linda, you and I writing lines for our end-of-year review, and pissing ourselves laughing at our own precocious wit. Elise, your school captain's righteous rage the day that Tim Foster broke into your prized Volkswagen, released the handbrake and rolled it out of sight. Discovering my hormones by the side of the basketball court one autumn lunchtime, watching Lin Piao dunking baskets in those non-regulation shorts. Miss Stewart summoning me to staff cottage—yet again—to ask me why I'd—yet again—moved out of home. Who knows how she discovered these things.

Now Elton John's singing me past Gerringong's vistas, and I can see that I'm still standing, and we're all looking like true survivors.

I'd love to share fond school-day memories with my now middle-aged school friends. But from the time I took that fateful taxi ride in 1988, life took me in a different direction.

3. the worst house in the best street

Back, for now, to 1978. In the summer holidays between primary and high school, I got a dog. I'd wanted one for years, and had been nagging Mum. I knew exactly what I wanted—an Old English sheepdog—and suddenly, there one was, in the Free column in the *Manly Daily* classifieds. He was in the pound.

Mum made me ask Dad, of course. And Dad wanted a return on this—he dictated a contract whereby I swore to adhere to ten conditions in return. There were clauses for walking and feeding the dog, keeping it clean, collecting and disposing of its poo. But I also had to wash the dishes every night, vacuum the house on weekends, and perform various other tasks—for the life of the dog, apparently.

The contract duly signed and witnessed, that Saturday morning Mum and I brought Jake home from Manly Dog Pound. I spent the rest of the weekend cutting away solid, dirty mats of fur with Mum's sewing shears to reveal a ribby, gangly, adolescent dog with doleful brown eyes. Jake trotted faithfully at our heels through the bush, around the streets, all that summer and for years thereafter.

I needed to take Jake to the local vet surgery within days of his arrival—he had some gastric infection, probably picked up at the pound—and I was immediately taken with the idea of being a veterinary surgeon. I asked if I could help out. And so started my first 'job'. I'd ride my dragster bike up the hill for a 7.30 am start. I had my own key. I cleaned out all the cages in the kennel room where dogs and cats stayed overnight, fed them, and walked any dogs that were well enough. Soon I was allowed to answer the phone and make appointments. In the consulting room I sat on a stool in the corner and watched, or sometimes held an animal still while the vet—big, brawny Terry Collins, with his ex-footballer's smashed nose—shaved a leg and took blood, or gave an injection, or administered a pill.

I loved the surgery, with its chequerboard linoleum floors and its smell of stainless steel, Chlorox and tiny white pills. When morning consultations were over I watched Terry performing surgery. And when school started again I sometimes turned up in the afternoons, just because I didn't want to go home. The nurses didn't seem to mind—bubbly, red-haired Narelle and even taciturn Lisa, who smoked and lived in the flat upstairs with her bikie boyfriend even though they weren't married.

In the May school holidays—I was in Year Seven—Terry asked me if I could fill in for Narelle for a week. It was a nurse's position and I would be paid. Flushed with pride, I raced the dragster down the hill to announce my news.

'Well, he'd better pay you a dollar an hour,' huffed Dad from behind *The Sun*.

When I got my first pay envelope, I found my hourly rate was $2.69. But it wouldn't have mattered to me what I was paid. I got to scrub up, wear a mask and pass instruments—scalpels, forceps, artery clamps—to the vets during surgical procedures. I adjusted the anaesthetic machine and monitored the animals as they woke up in their cages afterwards.

One afternoon after the vets had left for the day I scrubbed all the instruments, wrapped them into tidy green drape packages, placed them in the steriliser—really just a glorified pressure-cooker—and set the timer. While it burbled and hissed I continued with the other tasks—feeding the caged animals, swabbing down the tables, mopping the floor—then turned on the answering machine, locked up and went home.

In bed that night, I woke in a sweat at 2 am, heart thudding. Had I turned the steriliser off? I went over my movements again and again. I listened for sirens. I dozed, fitfully, until first light, then pedalled up the hill: there was the surgery, its glass frontage intact, not a wisp of smoke to be seen. I let myself in. The steriliser sat cold, its cycle long complete, on the bench beside the sink.

The responsibilities of having a real job were suddenly, scarily clear. But I had a purpose, a position and, I felt, respect in the practice. And I was only twelve! Perhaps, most of all, I had a place to go when home felt scary or unwelcoming. I would continue working at Seaforth Veterinary Hospital, on weekends and during school holidays, until I was seventeen and Terry could hire a qualified vet nurse for the same money. Anyway, by then the demands of the HSC had become my priority.

***

I started high school in 1978. I had attended 'Opportunity Class' at Neutral Bay Public School for years five and six. This was for kids who were doing well and might benefit from being extended into other areas of study. We learned recorder, did endless research projects, and had to present a short speech on an assigned topic every Monday afternoon, a prospect that had me camped in the girls' toilet every Monday lunchtime for two years. But Miss Sharp had noted and encouraged my creative writing, and when I won a full scholarship to SCECGS Redlands, a private school in Cremorne, she told Mum that it would have been the creative composition that caught the eye of the examiner.

I remember that exercise. We had to write about a photo reproduced on the exam paper. I stared at the photo, heart racing, until with just five minutes to go I worked out what it was—a street scene, blurry people with umbrellas, viewed from above through a wet windowpane, a smiling stick figure drawn into the condensation. I scribbled out a poem about the disconnect between the dismal, grey footpaths, the wet pedestrians and the smiley face.

So in 1978 I started high school at Redlands. My classmates were almost all from the suburbs of Sydney's affluent lower north shore—Northbridge, Castlecrag, Roseville. Redlands girls had smart houses with swimming pools and stay-at-home mothers. It's not that my parents were poor—Dad was Captain by then, on a decent wage, and Mum was teaching full-time—but Dad's hobby, property investment, was where he chose to spend his money. Our house in Seaforth was 'the worst house in the best street', a popular real estate dictum, a good investment. If Dad spent his money on plush carpets and modern bathrooms in his investment houses, he could charge more rent. But as for improving our family home, where was the return on that?

Despite this, Dad was very house-proud. When visitors arrived he would lead them from room to room, pointing out features: 'Now, this is the second bedroom, this one has a small built-in wardrobe … just here …' At first Jon, Matt and I would trail along to witness the visitors' appreciation of the linen press, or the *en suite* bathroom off the master bedroom, and share it anew. We would even take our own visitors on 'The Tour' on their first playdate. Soon, though, I realised the same favour was not being extended to me when I went to friends' houses, and I added it to my growing list of the peculiarities of Sangrado Street.

* * *

Now that Mum had her own money she set about trying to make our house more comfortable. She was paying off a new kitchen and some minor renovations. Clothing was never a priority, let alone fashion.

One day in Year Seven I met some friends in town to see a movie. The three of them looked me up and down. I read their faces; they were right, I looked embarrassing. I admit I was pushing my luck that day. Mum had bought me a pair of jeans—my first ever pair—but they were a couple of sizes too big (Mum was thrifty and always bought or made clothes too big, to get more years of wear out of them. The U-Sew-It summer tunic she made me in Year Seven was still too big for me in Year Twelve). I had tucked a hand-towel down my jeans, primarily to keep them up but also to create the illusion of hips. It hadn't worked. By unspoken agreement I followed ten paces behind my friends all day to spare their acute sensitivity.

When I got home, I told Mum that I needed some new clothes—and not specials from the discount table in Woolies. Mum said to ask Dad for some money and I found him typing a letter at his desk.

I take a deep breath. 'Dad, can I please have some money to buy clothes?'

Without taking his eyes from the typewriter he reaches into his pocket and thrusts some change at me.

I count it. $1.40. He laughs and starts typing again. When I get back to my bedroom, I stare at the handful of coins. It's too late to give it back.

* * *

The night before my first day at Redlands, Dad stopped me in the lounge room as I walked past his armchair.

'Jennifer, a word of advice.' He folded his newspaper in his lap and took a sip from his beer mug on the hearth.

I stopped still and held my breath.

'Don't make friends too fast. Hang back a bit and watch. Then, after a couple of years, you'll know who's who and you can decide who to buddy up with.'

I didn't know what to say.

'You understand? Otherwise you could get in with the wrong crowd.'

He picked his newspaper up again and I continued on my way.

* * *

'I was *hoping* to sit with you!' Caroline smiled cheerily as I sat down and put my books and pencil case on the desk. She had kind, grey eyes and lots of freckles. Hiding my delight, I heard myself explaining that I had asked the teacher if I could sit near the front of the class as I was short-sighted, but at the same time I was thinking, *How strange! How reckless of this girl to expose her feelings like that!*

Despite my reservations at her rashness, Caroline became my closest school friend, and soon we were absorbed into a little group of three pairs of girls. Our group of six remained closely aligned for the next few years. There were ambushes, encirclements, skirmishes and stand-offs—we were teenage girls, after all—but we were a clique, and I was a member. Sometimes they even appeared to like me. Maybe I was learning.

***

One Monday morning in Year Seven, Caroline was telling me what she'd done at the weekend. She said, 'We went to the beach'. Or maybe it was a picnic, or shopping, I can't remember now, because what struck me, even then, was that she had just assumed that I knew what 'we' meant—herself, her sister and her parents. Caroline had a firm sense of *belonging* in her family. Standing there in the corridor outside our homeroom, with other kids pushing past, chatting, I pondered how special that must feel.

4. all manner of unkindnesses

I may well have been earning $2.69 an hour at the vet clinic, but in Dad's eyes I was a failure, and my brothers too. One afternoon an acquaintance of Dad's arrived unannounced and we hadn't had time to make it to our rooms. Dad introduced us. 'That's Jennifer. She's long, isn't she? The one in the middle's Jonathan—he's blind in one eye. And the small one's Matthew. Not sure what's wrong with him yet.' He laughed.

Yes, okay, I was tall and thin. I hated it. But he didn't need to point it out to a stranger. I went numb and smiled.

Although Dad was physically violent from time to time, his verbal barbs were perhaps the cruellest for an adolescent girl. He'd remark on my looks, 'You're getting more pimples every day, Jennifer', or my prospects, 'You know you'll amount to nothing, don't you,' or, 'No boy will ever be interested in you'. These comments came out of nowhere, flung across the dining table or shot like darts as we passed in the hallway. He didn't even need to be drunk.

***

When I was very young, in my little-girl mind I was adopted. I daydreamed about my real family, the family I belonged to, who were frantically looking for me and would turn up at the door one day and say, 'She's ours and we want her back'. And I'd get in their car—it would be one with windows in the back seat so the kids could see out, not like our Holden Monaro—and drive away without a backwards glance.

But people were always saying how much I looked like Mum, so eventually I adjusted the fantasy slightly. Perhaps I had a real dad out there somewhere. This fantasy did cause me some difficulty because my mother, timid and exceedingly English-proper, was unlikely to have had an affair.

Still, I sometimes wondered if Mum would ever reveal my 'true' father's identity. Perhaps on her deathbed? 'Jen, dear, come closer,' she'd whisper from her pillow, beckoning weakly, and proceed to give me his name, and perhaps a clue or two so I could trace this man, who naturally would have always wondered about me and would greet me with tears of joy as I arrived on his doorstep.

OK, reality check. The man I call 'Dad' is my father. Live with it.

***

When I was thirteen I decided to stop speaking to Dad. I don't remember any particular event but I have a strong memory of thinking, *That's it. Enough.* When I tell people that, a common response is a wry smile and a suggestion of sexual abuse. A repressed memory, perhaps? I hardly think so. I remember all manner of unkindnesses; why would I repress just one? No, it was probably something not hugely significant in itself, just the last, spiteful straw.

Around that time I read in *The Sun* of the arrest of a woman who'd plotted with her son to kill her husband after years of his cruelty. I followed their story through the trial and her eventual acquittal. I didn't dare cut out clippings in case they could be used in evidence against me later on, should I ever need to act.

I'm sitting in the lounge room, watching the driveway, my new clutch bag in my lap. I'm in a new cotton skirt and short-sleeved blouse from the chain store boutique Katies—Elise helped me choose them—and new cream pumps that are already threatening to blister my heels.

I'm fifteen. A boy from church, two whole years older than me, has invited me to his end-of-year formal at St Andrews Cathedral School. He's picking me up—he has his own car. He said to be ready by 6 pm but now it's almost seven.

Dad keeps dropping by to chuckle mirthlessly and let me know that the invitation was a joke on me. 'Looks like he's changed his mind, eh, Jennifer? Eh? Eh?'

Mum used to tell me, 'Don't start crying until you get to your room. Don't let him know he's hurt you. Don't give him the pleasure.'

While Dad was at sea, I prayed nightly for a freak wave to sweep him from the deck of his ship. I was sure God would understand. In my darker moments, I had fantasies of bashing his bald dome with a house brick, again and again and again, sticky globs of brain and splinters of bone flying. I'd feel dizzy with power and relief.

At high school I continued to do well. At home I buried myself in study. I chose subjects like Latin, maths and sciences, where I was either right or wrong—no nuance, no ambiguity, no argument.

* * *

I'm in the backseat of the Monaro with my brothers. My eyes are shut tight. Dad's at the wheel. It's a wild, fast, frightening ride down Ponsonby Parade and I'm praying to God to move my cats off the driveway where they like to sun themselves. Wake up! Move! The car swerves to the left into Seaforth Crescent, then slams right into Sangrado Street, lurches right again and bounces across the gutter into Number Two. I open my eyes … blessed relief, no cats.

Then one day Duchess is there. A sickening bump-bump and a tabby and white blur streaks around the side of the house. By the time I find her there's blood coming from her mouth and her eyes. Dad's leaving for the Club so he offers me a lift to the vet surgery, Duchess limp on my lap in a towel, and drops me off in the carpark. 'I'll be in the main bar if you want a lift home.'

Duchess dies on the vet's white, Formica table a few minutes later.

I walk home.

* * *

Jon was fortunate in that Dad seemed to ignore him completely. But not Matt.

Matt hated peas. Rather than leave them on his plate, he would pick them up, one by one, over the course of his meal and poke them under the rim of his plate where they would only be discovered when Mum and I cleared the table. By then, he (and Dad) had usually left. But Dad must have caught on. One evening he lifted Matt's plate as Matt rose and exposed a neat circle of peas. The rest of us laughed but Dad slammed the plate down again, grabbed Matt and twisted his ear by the lobe. Matt would have been ten. I froze, furious but helpless. I could see Matt's eyes smarting, but he refused to cry. His kindergarten portrait surveyed the scene from the wall, a forced grin that his eyes didn't share, too sardonic for a five-year-old.

Dad's treatment has continued throughout Matt's adult life. He has harangued him, abused him and denigrated him in public. Eventually, when Matt's wedding approached, I told him that he didn't have to invite Dad.

'No, I will,' he said. 'I wouldn't want to invite that kind of karma on my marriage.' But at the reception there was no mention of Dad in Matt's speech.

Out of adversity comes … humour, often. In 1990 I was visiting Mum; Jon and Matt were both still living with her. I was 24, Jon 22 and Matt 17. There was a street fair on in Balgowlah and we decided to head there for a look around.

In the crowd Matt spotted Peter Garrett, lead singer of rock band Midnight Oil and local Balgowlah identity (as yet unblemished by politics), and hustled us all in his direction.

'Pete!' he said drawing near. 'I've got all the Oils albums!'

Garrett smiled his reluctant-teen-idol smile. 'Yeah, great, mate!'

But Matt wasn't finished. 'Look, Pete, I've got my family here, Mum and my brother and sister'—we smiled, obligingly. 'We don't all get together very often these days and I wonder if you'd do us a favour.' He grabbed Mum's camera from her (Mum always had a camera at the ready).

'Sure, no problem,' said Garrett, stepping forward to add himself to our little family tableau.

But Matt pushed the camera at him. 'No, mate, I mean, could you take a picture of us?'

Garrett stopped, blinked, then doubled over laughing. When he'd recovered, he stepped back, aimed the camera and clicked.

***

From the time I was fifteen, painful, sticky lesions started appearing between my fingers two days before Dad started every six-week leave. They would burst and weep, then clear up as soon as he went back to

Jen, Mum, Jon and Matt at a Balgowlah street fair (photo: Peter Garrett)

sea. I wrapped tissues around my throbbing fingers so I could hold a pen.

At night, Dad had the TV turned up high. He watched *Sale of the Century* after dinner and the sounds of gameshow buzzers, compere banter and audience applause echoed down the hallway to my bedroom. Whenever he went to the toilet I hurried to the lounge room and nudged the volume knob down a fraction. Luckily he went to the toilet often (all that beer), so within an hour or so I had the volume at an acceptable level without him suspecting a thing.

But there was always the chance of an argument at the dinner table, or some other major upset. And my School Certificate exams were about to start. I packed some clothes in a small suitcase and moved to Elise's house until the exams were over.

Girls talk, and one day I was called to the Staff Cottage verandah.

'Jenny, have you moved to Elise's house?' Our sweet, diminutive roll-call teacher had to look up at me.

'Yes, Miss Stewart.'

She narrowed her eyes. 'Is everything OK at home?'

Her sympathetic frown didn't tempt me, not for a minute. I grinned. 'Yes, Miss Stewart. We just thought we could help each other, studying for the exams together.' I hadn't needed to be told to lie. It was something to do with 'dirty laundry in public'—shame. I smiled cheerfully, hands in pockets to hide my sticky, tissue-swathed fingers, while Miss Stewart studied my face doubtfully.

* * *

As the years went on, Dad's lack of involvement in our lives took more and more toll. One night at dinner, a rowdy conversation revolved around the school day—Mum had a school day too, of course, which meant everyone except him.

'That's enough,' he said matter-of-factly, pushing some lamb chop and potato onto his fork. 'There'll be no more talk of school at this table.'

Dinner times were mostly silent affairs after that—apart from Jon's humming. We had little else to talk about.

* * *

My parents' relationship was distant at best. My father had always been very resentful of my mother's family, who he knew thought little of him. When he was drunk he would corner Mum and harangue her with grievances and perceived insults, sometimes for hours.

He often tried to undermine her professional confidence. 'You know you're a useless teacher. They all talk about it in the staffroom when you're not there.' In fact, Mum received accolades at school and in 2006 dozens of former colleagues and students would turn out for her funeral. But in those days, Mum would freeze, her eyes closed.

Mum is sitting at her end of the table, trying to finish her dinner, and Dad is bending over her. I observe the scene warily from the lounge room where my brothers and I are watching TV. He's closer than he ever gets, and saying, over and over, 'Your father killed your mother. Your father killed your mother. Your father killed your mother'. Mum tries to keep eating and doesn't say anything. She never answers back. 'Why don't you wake up to yourself?' he demands. 'Your father killed your mother. Your father killed your mother.'

Dad was also physically violent towards her—he gave her a black eye on one occasion. I was helping her cook dinner. Mum had placed the lid of the Sunbeam frypan on the (unlit) gas stove, a tea towel wrapped across it.

'Jesus! Get that towel off the stove!' Dad was drunk and Mum should have known he wasn't joking, but she smiled and playfully tossed the towel at him. That was enough. One quick stride and his hand flew out, slapping her hard enough to snap her head sideways. I just gaped. He was between us and the door and my knees went weak. But then he just grunted, turned around and went back to the TV. Mum went to her room and I finished dinner. By the morning her eye socket was ringed with purple and she had to go to school with it.

Jon and I could have been a support to each other during those years, except we'd never been close. We seemed to be in constant competition for Mum's attention. And, of course, Jon had his humming strategy. He'd been aware, though, of this incident. Later that night he stopped me outside the bathroom, eyes wide. 'Jen, Dad hit *Mum*!' He'd opened the way for us to talk about what was happening. And it's to my eternal shame that all I did was sneer and say, 'Yeah? So what? It's not the first time.' Then I turned on my heel and left him standing there. He would have been twelve, I fourteen.

I remember saying that—that it wasn't the first time—but now, all these years later, I'm not sure it was true. Perhaps I just needed to know more than him. Yet another arena of one-upmanship for me.

But my feelings for Jon were complicated.

I'm on 'The Long March', the church fellowship group's annual winter trek through the Blue Mountains. Jon has come along too this year and has wandered into a patch of nettles. A few others have gathered around him and an older girl—someone else's sister—is dabbing lotion on his legs. I hang around outside the circle, needing to be there but unable to go closer, confused at my feelings. Then I find a quiet spot outside the camp and cry.

* * *

Dad was an alcoholic, although I didn't realise it then. I thought that all fathers went to the RSL Club in the afternoon, arrived home, drank more beer then started on Scotch. I thought that Elise's dad was the weird one, interested and concerned for his kids' welfare. I thought all families dreaded hearing the car return from the Club. I believed Dad when he said it was Mum's fault that he drank too much, because he kept drinking until dinner and sometimes dinner wasn't ready until half past six.

There was always a bottle of Johnny Walker Red Label in the cupboard. One evening I stood in the kitchen with Mum, trying to empty the bottle down the sink, our hearts pounding, as Dad drove up the driveway. That's when I learnt that shaking a bottle doesn't make it empty any faster.

For years I studied in my room after dinner with the door cracked, half an ear on any conversation in the kitchen in case it turned nasty. I still don't know what I could have done, but something in me needed to know.

I asked Mum, later on, why she'd stayed with Dad. By then she was a Christian—when Dad left she started going to church. She closed her eyes. 'When I married your father I promised God that I would stay with him until death do us part.'

But there was more to it than that. Mum was a small child in London during World War II. She'd known poverty—and its shame—and would do anything to avoid it. Although her sister Julie was by then a single mother and coping, Mum believed that we were better off with Dad than without him.

Staying must have caused Mum huge internal conflict. She must have recognised the damage that living with an abusive father was doing to her children. But the fear of shame and poverty kept her—and by extension, us—there. When Dad eventually left, it took her a whole year to admit it to the neighbours.

* * *

Mum was very caring when it came to our education. She often sat up late helping me prepare for tests at school and even university exams—discussing endless questions, my notes spread around us, into the small hours when we would blearily retire, knowing I had the subject matter in hand.

When I search for other memories, examples of Mum's love, support or concern, I keep coming back to school matters. Sometimes we talked about Dad—usually teary, whispered exchanges. 'Ah, quit yer bawling,' Dad sneered at us once, returning to the kitchen where we were consoling each other after another nasty incident. 'Yer a couple of lezzos.' Mum and I stared at his departing back, then at each other, and crumpled with stifled laughter. But Mum never asked me about other aspects of my life. And although I spent much of my teenage years in a fog of confusion and depression, I never went to her with my worries—about falling out with friends, for instance, or being bullied, or trouble with teachers.

One day in the playground in Year Eleven, I was sitting with a small circle of friends, pulling out small clumps of my hair. I can't remember why. I couldn't have said why at the time. It just felt good. Lia, one of the popular girls, stood up and walked off, tossing 'You're *sick*!' over her shoulder. She was probably right. Was this my own small stand, a petty effort at self-harm?

In the main, I felt that any problem I was having reflected my own deficiencies more than anything else, and there was no way in the world I was going to lay those bare, even for Mum. No, *especially* for Mum. Perhaps, like a lot of things, it comes back to shame. I knew Mum was ashamed of me and I wasn't going to give her more reason if I could help it.

* * *

I have tried many times to write about Mum in a lucid, narrative flow. And failed.

So here's a series of disparate vignettes and memories in no particular order, unrelated fragments of a life.

When I was a toddler and there was a skywriter, Mum would put me outside on a rug with my plastic letter set. My task was to match the letters with the ones in the sky. Then when the aeroplane had droned off, and the hazy forms had dissolved into the ether, she would come out and decipher for me the pilot's message.

When I started menstruating at fourteen I felt I should let Mum know. With a heady mixture of excitement, trepidation and embarrassment, I dropped my stained undies into the washing basket on the afternoon of that first day. Mum did a load of washing every night and was assiduous about spraying stains with Preen, so I waited for her to say something. Nothing.

Relieved to find that—as *Dolly*, a magazine for teenaged girls, had foretold—these things started slowly, I did the same the next day. Still nothing from Mum. On the third day I worked through my mortification and asked Mum if she could give me some sanitary pads. Red-faced and silent, she led me to her bedroom and handed me a bulky packet from the dim, naphthalene-spiked recesses of her wardrobe.

Soon I wanted to start using tampons. I cut out and posted off a coupon from a Tampax ad in *Dolly* and soon a sample pack in brown paper arrived in the post. That night in the bathroom, armed with the instruction leaflet and a jar of Vaseline, I managed to get one in.

I had to tell someone. I found Mum at the stove, cooking dinner. I took a deep breath. 'Mum, I've got a tampon in.'

Mum froze and stared at me. 'But ... but you're not *married*!'

A few years later, Mum was appointed the sex education teacher at her school. One morning, chuckling softly, she packed a raw zucchini into her lunchbox. 'I have to show the students how to put on a condom!' she explained. I was surprised and impressed at her new role. This was the woman who had a row of pots on the kitchen windowsill—her cactus collection. She'd given them all names.

'This one's Barb, and this one's Spike,' she'd tell visitors proudly. 'And this one's Prick.'

Prick was one of those cactuses that had started as a spiny little knob but had grown longer and longer. Jon and I would snort into our fists and the visitor would look from face to face, unsure whether to laugh.

One day Dad came towards me in the kitchen with his hand raised after I'd answered back. I was twelve.

Mum sprang between us. 'Don't hit her!' she squeaked, bouncing up and down, 'Hit me, hit *me*!' I'd never seen her like that. Dad muttered something and left the room.

I suspect that Mum had an attraction to a certain kind of man. Amongst the many boyfriends of mine that she met over the years, there were only two that she heartily approved of. They were certainly charming ... but both, like Dad, were addicts.

Mum told me that she used to cry when she breastfed me. She wasn't sure why, but, 'then I'd be worried it would harm you, which would make me cry more'.

When I was in my twenties and had returned from Pune, I started hugging Mum when we met. We'd never hugged before. Mum was reticent at first but soon took to this new greeting and would cling limpet-like, for longer than was comfortable. I would wait a while then extricate myself. Besides, she smelled a bit funny—a mixture of moth balls and Oil of Ulan.

Mum was a special education teacher. She worked at a school for children with physical disabilities, and many of them had terminal illnesses.

For years she taught George, who had a congenital bone condition. He was very small and prone to breakages and was brought to school every day on a custom-designed cot. I met him once; he had a great sense of humour.

Long Road to Dry River

When George died, at sixteen, Mum grieved as for a child of her own. Years later, I was looking through a photo album, a 'Family' album—Mum always sorted photos rigorously, and any photo containing anyone without a blood tie was designated 'Friends'. But there in a 'Family' album was George, in his cot, grinning at the camera.

One day, as a teenager, I was looking for an envelope and opened a drawer in Mum's desk. In there I found a sheaf of notepaper filled with Mum's tiny, neat, school-teacher cursive. It began, 'Well, girl, you've really gone and done it this time.' I read a few more lines then hid the pages under some exercise books and closed the drawer. I can't remember what else I read. What I do remember is my veins turning to ice.

Around my friends, when she visited me in Quaama, Mum used to wear her sunglasses, all the time. Even inside.

After Mum died, Auntie Julie and I went to pack up her bedroom. In her chest of drawers we found a collection of bars of soap—special soaps, dozens of them—still in their wrapping. Gifts over the years from students? We opened a couple. No scent left at all. And a bar of plain, budget-price Dove beside the basin in her bathroom.

One day, long after Mum died, Flavienne said, 'You were always the favourite.'

'Really?' I said.

'Yes. Betty used to say, "How could someone like me have made someone like Jen?"'

Anyway, Flavienne took that to mean pride.

On the day in Manly Hospital when the nurses told us that Mum was dying, but she was still conscious, we took turns to say good-bye. Jonathan went first.

'I love you, Mum,' he said.

'I love you too, darling.'

Then Matt. 'I love you, Mum.'

'I love you too, darling.'

Auntie Julie. 'I love you, Betty.'

'I love you too, Julie.'

My turn. 'I love you, Mum.'

'Thank you, dear.'

The first Christmas after Mum's death, I drove south from a family gathering in Sydney, detoured inland to visit my school friend Caroline on her property at Araluen, then continued. On my way back to the coast it occurred to me that, for perhaps the first time in my life, no-one in the world would be wondering where I was.

5. what kind of family was *this*?

One afternoon on the 714 school bus a kind-looking boy from a private school in North Sydney gave up his seat for me. I was fifteen. Naturally I fell in love that minute. His name was Malcolm and he lived in Seaforth too. Another afternoon soon after that, Malcolm suggested I come to a youth fellowship meeting at St Paul's Anglican Church. And so it was that I fronted up at the church hall at seven o'clock that Friday night, and every Friday night for the next few years.

There was always a good crowd, perhaps thirty teenagers and a handful of twenty-somethings to keep us in line. There were prayers, a talk by one of the older youths, and games—the kind of games that teach life lessons. In one memorable one, we had messages pinned to our backs. The message might say, 'Reject me if I'm taller than you' or, 'Accept me if my eyes are the same colour as yours' or even, 'Always reject me' or, 'Always accept me'. We'd mill around, reading the messages on each other's backs and accepting or rejecting each other accordingly. The aim was to form groups, and as a group became larger, complying with all the members' prerequisites became harder. We didn't know what our own message said—we just knew if we'd been accepted or not. In the end there'd be large groups and smaller ones and maybe some pairs and always a few hapless singles. Then we'd have a debrief and talk about what it felt like to be accepted or rejected.

But one thing about Christians is that they accept everyone—it's a point of honour. I suddenly had a social life, lots of friends, two regular outings per week (okay, one of them was the Sunday evening church service but a group of us from fellowship went to Philippe's Crepes on Sydney Road afterwards for coffee) and parties at least once a month. And the parties were great. Elton John, Queen, Adam Ant, Lionel Richie … I danced all night.

It turned out that Malcolm had a girlfriend already. Her name was Lynn, and we became firm friends. We spent weekend afternoons sprawled on the lounge room floor, learning the lyrics to all the songs on Meatloaf's 'Bat out of Hell' album—we even had word-perfect the metaphorical baseball commentary from *Paradise by the Dashboard Light*. Our friendship was only dulled a little when, one rainy Saturday afternoon, we went driving in Lynn's dad's Volvo—she was a year older than me and she'd got her license. She offered me a turn, and I skidded round a gravelly corner on a quiet, well-to-do Seaforth street, panicked, accelerated instead of braking and took out a parked car and a brick wall. No-one was injured but I was summoned to Manly Police Station the following week and cautioned. Dad was furious—he said I should have done time in a girls' home.

But there was another boy at St Paul's youth fellowship meetings—Graeme. Graeme lived just a short walk from our house, although I'd never met him before. He became my first boyfriend.

One night I was at dinner with Graeme's family. His mother, father and three sisters were at the table. Laura, a few years older than Graeme, would soon be married and would move to Adelaide where her husband-to-be, Geoff, had been offered a job at the university. There was much excited speculation about her new life until one by one everyone fell silent: Faith, the youngest at thirteen, was crying.

The others started telling her, 'It's OK, Faith, we'll visit!' ... 'And they'll come back for Christmas!' Then Graeme's father stood up from his seat at the end of the table, walked slowly round to Faith's chair, and silently wrapped his arms around her.

At this, I burst into tears and stumbled from the room. I wasn't even close to Laura, or Faith, for that matter; it wasn't that. I was overcome with feelings I couldn't even start to identify. At the table, unabashed emotion had evoked loving concern and consolation, a father's overt display of love. What kind of family was *this*?

***

One day I was in science class when the PA crackled. Usually someone was being summoned to Staff Cottage for a misdemeanour, and the same names would crop up again and again. I was concentrating on the report I was writing when Elise poked me in the ribs. When I looked up, everyone was staring at me, goggle-eyed. It seemed that today was my day. And it was no less than the headmaster, PJ Cornish, wanting a word.

I hurried downstairs and along the playground to the Cottage, mentally working my way through the last few days, but came up with nothing. Still, I'd broken out in a light sweat. PJ? This must be serious.

Waiting on the verandah were PJ and Miss Stewart. I searched her face for a clue. Was she trying not to *smile*?

PJ commenced proceedings. 'Jenny, we've had a call from a Miss Briggs.'

Oh, *her*, I thought. She and her mother owned the corner store in Seaforth. I used to stop there sometimes for a chocolate bar after getting off the bus in the afternoon. But what now? I hadn't been rude. I certainly hadn't shoplifted. Surely she hadn't reported me for eating in school uniform?

'Yes, Mr Cornish?'

But now even PJ was smiling. 'Jen, you'll have to be more discreet. Miss Briggs thought the school may be interested in how close you and a certain, ah …' he raised one eyebrow, '*paramour* … stand at the bus stop in the mornings'.

The prudish old busybody! The store wasn't even open at that hour—she must have been watching from her adjoining house. But it was true. I'd be sitting on the brick wall in the morning sun, reading a book, when I'd hear the soft whirr of Graeme's racing bike approaching. Then he'd be there, in his crisp white shirt, his Balgowlah Boys' High navy King Gee shorts and desert boots, smelling of fresh sweat, and … I tore my attention back to Staff Cottage, the heat rising in my face. Miss Stewart was smiling now and patting my arm—I could swear she looked proud. If there was a girl in our year least likely to be caught in a compromising situation it was probably me, and we all knew it.

'The dowagers of Seaforth must be appeased!' said PJ, and wandered off, chuckling.

I tried, I really tried, to behave a little more decorously with Graeme after that. But it didn't do my reputation any harm at all, when the story got out. And it got out as soon as I got back to the science lab, of course.

* * *

Year Eleven at Redlands saw the arrival of Dharmendra and Lin Piao, from Johor Bahru, Malaysia—among Redlands' first forays into overseas student enrolments. They were tall, athletic and handsome. They were witty and urbane. They were *fun*.

We immediately absorbed Dhar and Piao into our schoolday activities and our weekend social program. They were boarding at the home of the school's Chairman in Manly Vale and Graeme and I would swing past to pick them up in Graeme's Ford Escort panelvan, where they'd cling desperately and hilariously to any handhold they could find on the back tray on the way to barbecues and parties.

One day in Year Twelve basketball practice was in session on the school courts. I was watching Lin Piao in his tight shorts and realised with a pang that I no longer regarded him just as a friend. But I had a boyfriend, it was my HSC year—the last thing I needed was romantic complications. My strategy was to say nothing, suffer my crush in silence, and write reams of dreadful poetry. So much for that. It wasn't long before Piao cornered me by the lockers in the stairwell.

He was trying to enlarge his eyes with the thumb and first finger of each hand.

I stared at him. 'Piao, are you OK? What's wrong with your eyes?'

'I want you to know my feelings, Jenny! I'm afraid you can't see my soul!' Piao had lovely, brown, almond-shaped eyes, typical of his Chinese heritage. I started to giggle and he dropped his hands. 'Last night I started so many letters to you. But I could not express my feelings. The wastepaper bin in our bedroom is full of them—so much scrunched up paper. So now all I have is my words. I love you!'

'Oh, Piao,' I said, 'I love you too!' Well, it was lust, at least.

It was terribly romantic. But I was a good, church-going girl and had sworn myself to Graeme. And Piao and Graeme had become friends too. I told him that our love would have to remain platonic. Then I went home and wrote reams of dreadful poetry anyway.

* * *

At school, my favourite subject was Latin. For the HSC I took the highest level I could, 3-Unit, and immersed myself in Cicero, Ovid and Vergil. I loved the almost mathematical certainty of translations. Between tenses, voices, moods and the rest, every Latin verb had 128 endings, and there were similar distinctions when declining nouns. There could be no argument about what an ancient Roman had meant.

I wanted to continue with Latin at university but Mum said, 'No, do something practical. You have to be able to support yourself.' I'm not sure now if she meant that I should never need to depend on a man, as she did—or believed she did. But I took her advice. Instead of applying for ancient languages at some sandstone edifice with soft green lawns and hushed libraries, I enrolled at an institute of technology. In 1984 I started a Biomedical Science degree at what is now the University of Technology, Sydney, a solid vocational course in life sciences that would qualify me to work in a pathology laboratory.

That first year I met Simon, a passionate, funny, extroverted boy doing the same degree. We were friends all year, then as summer came on things became more serious.

At the same time, Graeme and I were having problems. After my HSC exams the previous year we'd taken a road trip across the country to visit my

German schoolfriend Urte, who had moved to Perth with her parents the previous year. We took Graeme's little Ford Escort panel van—ambitious, yes. When we got back, after six weeks, the church fellowship community gave us an icy reception. Had we had sex? I can't remember anyone asking us outright, but the whispers got back to us. I'll leave you to decide for yourself—two healthy eighteen-year-olds on a six week unchaperoned holiday? But even if we hadn't, we were charged, tried, convicted ... and ostracised. So much for belonging. Graeme decided to join a different church in a neighbouring suburb and wanted me to come with him. But I was losing interest—in Graeme *and* the church.

There was something else. Graeme had been very upset when I got my HSC results—lower than his *but not by enough*. Too close, in his eyes, for comfort. A few months later he took me out to Palm Court Chinese Restaurant in Balgowlah for a celebratory dinner. Over the crispy lemon chicken, special fried rice and glasses of Mateus Rosé he revealed the occasion: he'd 'got over' my mark. I wasn't sure exactly whom he'd forgiven—me or the Board of Senior School Studies. But it was an awakening of sorts for me. Was *Girls in Pink*, my gloomy, feminist Year Ten poem, prophetic of the future available to me in this relationship? We struggled on for the rest of the year, while Simon hovered.

I broke up with Graeme as considerately as I could; I waited until after his end-of-year law exams. That meant waiting until after my exams too. That semester I had five subjects: one exam every morning for a week. I developed temporary anorexia, managing to get down just one banana each day. I stayed awake studying all night and fretting about giving Graeme the word, before heading into town, doing my exam and returning home to fall into bed and sleep all afternoon—then studying again all night for the next day's exam. Then I told Graeme it was over. He'd met Simon and took it as badly as I expected, but after that my appetite returned. A month later I got my results—five distinctions (I would never manage to replicate those results in my remaining university years).

Simon was an avid fan of the funky, flamboyant, androgynous artist Prince, whose album 'Purple Rain' was released that year. One night I'd watched him boogie on a table at the university bar to *Baby, I'm a Star*. He wore a tight black suit, white wing-tip collar and purple cummerbund. But that Saturday, Simon and I danced cheek-to-cheek to the slow, dreamy title track in the lounge room of his father's rental in Campsie. It may have been my first time in Sydney's western suburbs.

Graeme had once said to me, 'You'll never win a beauty competition but I love you anyway'. At the time I thought that was the height of devotion. But Simon loved me *and* found me attractive. I learned to look in the mirror. I had my ears pierced, got my hair cut and permed (never again) then started spending the little money I had on attractive clothes.

***

During the next year I started experiencing pain in my right side, and our family doctor diagnosed a kidney infection and prescribed antibiotics. But the infection kept returning so he referred me to a specialist. One winter afternoon in his rooms in St Leonards I found myself staring at a scan of my pelvis, and by then I'd learned enough about anatomy to see for myself that something was wrong—whereas my left kidney was big and healthy, the right one was tiny.

'It's about the size of a five-year-old's,' the nephrologist told me. 'That's when it must have stopped growing. It's causing too much trouble—we'll have to take it out.'

But I was in the middle of a demanding academic year. 'Can it wait until December?'

He sighed. 'I suppose so, but you'll be on antibiotics until the operation.' We scheduled surgery for the week after my exams, and I finished the year constantly clutching my right side.

A couple of years beforehand, Dad had told Mum he didn't want to pay for health insurance anymore. 'We'll carry our own insurance,' he'd said. But Mum wasn't as confident, and had secretly opened a policy for the family with the Teachers Federation fund. So as my procedure approached, a dilemma weighed upon her: if she told Dad about the operation, it would open up a discussion about how to pay for it, and her insurance policy would come to light.

We decided he didn't need to know.

In November, Dad announced that he was going to have a party. It was the first party he'd ever hosted. 'The first of December looks good,' he said. It was a Sunday, and I was due at Royal North Shore Hospital for surgery the next morning at seven o'clock.

'Lovely!' said Mum.

So the evening of 1 December saw a house full of guests at Sangrado Street. Well, reasonably full—Dad didn't have a lot of friends, and most of the guests were Mum's family, friends or colleagues. Johnny Mathis and George Benson were on the turntable and Mum was passing around platters of French onion dip with Jatz crackers, or cheese cubes and cabanossi rounds with toothpicks, a rictus-tight smile across her face, practically humming with tension. All the family and Mum's work friends knew about my operation the next day, and the secrecy around it, and I remember a number of hushed, wide-eyed conversations, always watching for Dad. But we needn't have worried. Dad was off conducting tours of the house for much of the night.

Of course he was going to find out eventually, but I suspect Mum just wanted to get the operation out of the way before she decided how to deal with that. I would be in hospital for ten days—plenty of time, she thought, to find some excuse for her subterfuge. But when she got home late the next day, spent and emotional after six hours waiting with Simon for me to emerge from theatre, Dad confronted her.

'What's this about an operation, Betty? Some doctor at North Shore Hospital rang. I think I managed to bluff my way through the conversation but it was very embarrassing!'

The surgeon hadn't been able to find Mum when he left the operating theatre—she and Simon had been waiting at the wrong door, it seemed—so he'd called the number on my admission form.

I'm not sure what Mum told Dad then, but she didn't reveal the insurance policy. I know that, because a couple of years later Dad needed a minor procedure of his own, and Mum gleefully maintained her secret; he footed the entire bill himself. After all, he'd carried his own insurance.

***

Reliving this story, and Mum's mendaciousness, I wonder now about another motivation. I've said that Dad was uninvolved in our lives. He'd become quite isolated by this time. Would he have been concerned if he'd known about my impending operation—if Mum had told him? I do remember that he seemed less antagonistic towards me during my early convalescence. Not kind or caring by any stretch, but not so cruel either.

Sometimes I wonder if Mum chose to exclude him, as much as he excluded himself.

One day, years later, I had Mum in the car. We were driving over the Harbour Bridge when I revealed to Mum that I was talking to Dad—that we were trying to build a relationship of sorts. She was quiet for a while, then she said, 'You know, one day when you were going out to meet some friends, you were wearing a yellow dress, and it was quite see-through. After you'd gone—he was watching you walk down the driveway—he said that he hoped you'd get raped. That you needed to be taught a lesson, dressing like that.'

Looping down onto the Cahill Expressway, I remembered that yellow dress. I'd saved up my pay from the vet surgery to buy it. It was lemon-coloured cheesecloth, with cap sleeves, a long, full skirt and embroidery across the bodice. I imagined myself heading out that day, the fabric light and breezy around my legs. Now, my twenty-eight-year-old heart squeezed for that fourteen-year-old me, who didn't have a full length mirror.

I understood—*He's the bad parent*, Mum was saying. *Remember, I'm the good one.* But she hadn't said anything that day. She'd let me go out in a see-through dress.

* * *

Mum's advice to study a practical course at university was prescient. I did have to support myself, and sooner than I expected. As I gained strength again after my operation, Dad's nasty jibes were gearing back up and Simon was unhappy living with his father too. When I'd recuperated sufficiently we started planning to get our own place. First we got jobs. Simon found a lab assistant position at a pharmaceutical company in Ermington and I started as an electroencephalography technician (yes, that one really had eyes glazing over at parties) with a group of neurologists in St Leonards. Then we signed a lease on a flat in Top Ryde, about halfway between our two workplaces.

At Sangrado Street, Mum stood on the balcony and cried as we backed down the driveway with my old wardrobe occy-strapped onto a hastily-constructed set of roof racks on Simon's 1969 Mercedes, and a few bags of my clothes, books and records in the backseat.

She would tell them in the staffroom, if they asked, that I was 'flatting with a friend'—the shame again. Dad, who was gardening in the front yard, kept weeding along the side fence with his back to us. He'd told Mum to demand the return of my house key ('for security'). Mum later gave it back to me, but I only ever visited when I knew Dad was at sea.

During the next two years I completed my degree at night. By day I recorded brainwave traces for the neurologists, applying electrodes to patients' scalps to produce charts of wriggly, magenta lines on graph paper. Soon the wriggly lines started to make sense. I knew that the worried patients' brains were more likely to exhibit the faster beta-waves. And the more relaxed patients' brains would feed slower alpha waves onto my chart. But the neurologists weren't interested in that. Often they wanted to know about any classic, conclusive 'spike-and-wave' discharges that would pepper the traces of epileptic patients. If epilepsy was suspected and I didn't see any convincing spikes during the regular program I would shine a flickering light in the patient's eyes to see if I could invoke one. If I then saw a spike-and-wave I had to turn the light off immediately or take the chance of inducing a full-blown seizure.

The slower, symmetrical theta waves could simply indicate that the patient was falling asleep. After all, the chair was very comfortable. But they might mean a serious pathological event, if they occurred only on one side of the brain.

Soon the neurologists trusted me to write preliminary reports. If there were quiet times I could study at my desk. Then at five o'clock I gathered my books and went to my classes at the campus where Simon and I studied, a short walk through the Royal North Shore Hospital grounds across the road.

It was during a microbiology lecture one night in my final year that I looked up at the whiteboard and found that I had, from one moment to the next, lost the lower half of the field of vision in my right eye. 'That's strange,' I thought. The next day at work I mentioned it to one of the neurologists, who referred me to an ophthalmologist in our building. But by the time of my appointment, a few days later, my vision had returned to normal. The ophthalmologist examined my eye, said he couldn't see anything wrong, and suggested I come back if it happened again. It would be ten years before I gave it another thought.

6. a reckoning

Simon and I were happy in our Top Ryde flat. We'd made friends with a couple in the block next door; they were tennis players like Simon, so he joined the local club. Simon was a talented but passionate player and smashed too many racquets for our meagre household budget. But tennis opened up a new social circle for us. We spent Saturday mornings at the courts, had boozy lunches at the beer barn nearby with the team, then drove home and spent the rest of the weekend recovering—unless we had Sunday lunch with Sonny, Simon's father, and his girlfriend Sue in Coogee, where we'd drink too much again. Black Russians were my poison when Sonny was paying, and I took the Kahlua and vodka mix straight, with ice. None of that fizzy stuff for me.

But in 1988, after two years living on low wages, we wanted more. We had our degrees. We bought the newspaper every Saturday and trawled through the Positions Vacant columns. Sales jobs were where the money was.

I got lucky first, getting a position with a small company in Crows Nest. I swapped my white clinician's uniform for smart suits and a briefcase to sell cardiac equipment to cardiologists and intensivists. The salary was much higher than an electroencephalographer's and there was a generous car allowance, with which I was paying off a silver Holden Commodore station wagon. I started travelling interstate too. It was the first time I'd flown, and I really felt that I was making it in the world.

Simon got a job with a scientific instrumentation company, but he was an assistant in the sales department rather than a sales representative. He helped the reps prepare their promotional materials and set up stalls at trade fairs. It was a step up from where he'd been but it didn't have the prestige of my position. For the first time, tensions arose between us. I was travelling a lot, and Simon started drinking—alone.

One evening in May I arrived home from a sales trip. Simon was still at work. I turned on the light to be greeted by two lists written on the balcony doors. Simon had daubed a reckoning into the condensation the night before, and it had been preserved by the dust. We weren't the most attentive housekeepers.

On the plus side, I learned, I was 'beautiful'. On the minus, 'boring'. I pored through the lists. Some items were surprising, but I agreed with much of it.

Soon he told me he was moving out.

Simon has signed a lease on a flat in Chatswood. I have to tell Mum, who thinks we're getting married—otherwise how could I, in all conscience, be sharing a bed with him? I drive over to Mum's house and find her in her office, typing up a program for the coming school term on the MicroBee computer she lugs home from school every Friday afternoon.

I flop onto the spare bed behind her. 'Mum, Simon's moving out.'

Mum keeps typing, silently.

My voice catches. 'He says he's just not happy anymore.'

Mum's still typing.

I pick up my keys and drive back home.

* * *

A sales trip to Melbourne, a taxi ride on a rainy night ... Pune, Melbourne, the Hoffman Process ... and a flight to Sydney to visit my long-estranged father.

Part Three

1. whose was the payout?

May 1994. My parents had divorced since I'd moved away. Mum was still in Sangrado Street with my brother, Matthew, and my father was living on his own, back in Balgowlah. He'd announced he was moving out—he'd bought another house, unbeknown to Mum—the week before Matt's HSC exams started in 1990. In his defence, he probably didn't know about Matt's exams (not much of a defence, I know). He'd offered Mum thirty percent of the marriage assets. When Mum's solicitor asked, during mediation, 'Why not fifty percent?' Dad said, 'She took ten years off work!' It was true. She was raising his children.

I looked him up in the phone book and called him, my heart thudding.

'Dad? It's Jennifer.'

A few seconds silence. 'Jennifer…'

I shivered. 'I'd like to come and visit, if that's OK with you?'

Another pause. 'Yeah. Of course.' He sounded curious, if not friendly.

We agreed on a time the following day. I engaged the help of a friend, who would wait in the car outside. I'm not sure if I was still frightened of my father's violence, and if it had come to that, what use would a friend in a car in the street be? But it felt good to have someone nearby.

I rang the doorbell and the latch clicked immediately—he must have been waiting there; he'd seen me arrive. He wore khaki trousers, left-over uniform from his sailing days, and a bulky orange cardigan that I thought I remembered Mum knitting. He was balder, shorter, thinner. He gave me 'The Tour', as if I were interested in his new house. He asked me if I wanted tea, biscuits, lunch … he seemed nervous. 'Just tea, thanks,' I said.

I was probably in the house for an hour. We sat at a table in a bright little sunroom with leadlight windows. I told him about the Hoffman Process and the things I'd learned. I told him a little about my life, and he spoke a little about his view of my childhood.

'I wasn't very paternal, I know. Maybe because *my* father wasn't paternal,' he said.

I was surprised at Dad's insight. And when he said, 'I never really wanted kids,' I was touched by the admission.

We talked about his relationship with Mum.

'She wouldn't argue,' he said. 'She'd give me the silent treatment when she was angry. I hated that. There wasn't anything I could do.'

I remembered Mum's tight, closed face and the silence. It could last for days. By now I recognised it as classic 'passive aggression'. I'd learned well—it was a tactic I'd employed in my early relationships too. I could have Simon in tears, stamping his feet, by day three.

I reminded myself why I was there, then looked him in the face.

'Well, I love you,' I said. It wasn't true, but that was the assignment. Dad looked out the window, and his eyes were red around the rims and a bit moist. But alcoholics often have moist, red-rimmed eyes. He didn't answer.

In the three years that followed I visited Sydney every few months. That year for my birthday Dad gave me a copy of *Love You to Bits and Pieces*, by Gillian Helfgott. I wondered if this was his clumsy way of telling me he loved me. Then again, it may just have been something he spotted on the bookshop remainders table.

Although there had never been any physical affection in my family, least of all from Dad, he took to hugging me, roughly, when we met.

We're at Manly Beach, Mummy and Daddy, Jonathan and I. I'm six. It's an ocean beach so Mummy doesn't go in the water, she's too scared of rips. Daddy always goes right out the back, behind the waves, where the water is deep and dark and dangerous.

Daddy stands up to go in the water, and I ask him if he can take me too. Mummy says, Brian, please hold onto her.

He mutters something but he hasn't said no, so I follow him to the water's edge. We wade out through the first few small waves then he swings me up onto his back. He starts to swim and I'm holding on. I get scared and put my arms around his neck but he shouts at me, You're choking me! *So I try to hold onto his shoulders but they're wide and slippery with suntan oil, and they churn with the strokes of his arms through the waves. My small hands can't grip. I'm sliding off and grabbing at him, and he's shouting at me:* Jennifer, for Christ's sake, hold on! *He won't hold me; he won't touch me with his hands.*

* * *

When I visited, Dad always took me out to dinner—Asian food was his preference—but he drank heavily and our meals were never pleasant. It seemed my initial visit had deflected his ill-feeling away from me and onto other family members. By dessert he was always red-faced and ranting about his treatment by Mum's family, and I would create some excuse for leaving. On the first occasion I'd parked at his house and allowed him to drive us both to the restaurant. He insisted on driving back, quite drunk, and after that I always drove myself.

On one visit, maybe wanting to share his hobbies with me, Dad took me to Seaforth RSL Club and led me to the smoky poker machine area, with its tinny, cartoonish melodies and air of spilled beer.

Dad changed a fifty dollar note for one dollar coins and headed for a machine in the corner. 'This is the luckiest machine,' he explained.

'Watch this, Jennifer. This is the lucky way of feeding the coin,' he said, pushing a dollar into the slot. 'And this is the lucky way to pull the lever.' The machine burbled, the cards spun, a row of hearts and spades and clubs rolled into position. No luck. He fed another coin: again, no winnings.

I'd been watching carefully. 'Can I have a go?'

He looked at me, hesitated, then handed me a few coins.

I fed the machine a coin as he had, then pulled the lever as he had. A trill of jeering music. No pay. I repeated the process. Still no luck.

Dad's hands darted for the lever. 'No, no, no,' he said. 'Give me the coins back.' I moved aside and let him take over.

It was only later that I realised what his discomfort was: if I'd won, and brought the cascade of coins ringing and crashing into the tray below, it would have raised an awkward question: whose was the payout?

* * *

One day in 1996 I received a call from Dad on my mobile. I was in a check-out queue at a supermarket in Melbourne and asked if I could call him back, but he was quite excited and would not be put off.

'The thing is, Jennifer, I'd like to see you in your own place. It's about time you owned some property. I've got a spare $50,000 and I want to lend it to you for a deposit—at low interest, of course.' By this time Dad owned a few residential and commercial properties. I fumbled with my purse and paid the cashier.

'Without property you're nothing,' he said. He was very uncomfortable with the fact that I was renting. As for me, I'd always rented and was quite happy to continue. And I'd left Domedica and was running my own small business (okay, *very* small business) so the banks wouldn't exactly be queuing up to offer me a mortgage. But I thanked him for the offer, and tucked it away in the back of my mind.

Over the next few months Dad continued to press me accept the loan. His next tactic was to say that he had $100,000 to spare so could extend the offer to two of the three of us siblings; none of us owned property yet. There was never the thought of dividing the money three ways. Dad had a history of making us compete.

I'm in the kitchen one morning making myself breakfast. I'm eleven. Dad and Jon are at the table. I have carefully buttered a piece of toast and spread it with strawberry jam. I return the butter and jam to the fridge, and when I turns around there's a perfect bite out of the corner of my toast, and Dad is laughing.

Jonathan's chewing furiously. He looks petrified. He takes off and I chase him, out the back door, round the side of the house to the gate. He's halfway over the gate when I catch his ankle and rake it with my nails.

When I get back inside, I go to my room. Dad follows me in, kicks me hard on the leg and leaves. It's a few minutes before I can stand up and there will be a big, black bruise on my thigh for weeks.

***

But this time Dad's strategy didn't work. I rang Jon and Matt to check and none of us was keen to take up the offer. We all agreed that there would be strings attached. Tangled, knotty strings.

What changed my mind was my first trip to Quaama, a small town of 150 or so inhabitants—really just a village—on the banks of Dry River, north of Bega, on the far south coast of New South Wales. It was May 1997.

In Pune, while I ran the Hygiene Department, an Australian sannyasin called Neehar had liaised with local farmers to supply fresh, healthy produce for the ashram, so we'd worked together and become friends. And now I was working with him again, but in a very different capacity; this time he was liaising with a silversmith factory in Pune to produce rings, earrings and pendants from our original designs—some New Age, some gothic—and, for my part, I got to sit in tiny shops in Jaipur's old Johari Bazaar while men in white pyjamas strew rainbows of semi-precious stones across white cotton mattresses around me—amethysts, tourmalines, turquoise, lapis lazuli, aquamarines. I picked through them for the choicest gems to feature in our Tree of Life Pendants or our Spider Web Earrings. Then, when each shipment arrived in Melbourne, I'd visit the new age bookshops and the gothic boutiques and fill orders.

Neehar and his partner Nirda had rented a small farmhouse on *Illawambra*, a property northwest of

Quaama (pronunciation tip: 'it's warmer in Quaama')—Neehar had lived on a commune in the area in the 1970s and now they were living between *Illawambra* and Pune while they looked for a property to buy. Many members of that original commune, Tralfamadore, had ended up in Pune and had now come back to the Far South Coast. Neehar's sister Sangito lived in Quaama; others had settled around Bermagui on the coast.

Now Neehar had invited me to stay for a few days. The trip would be a nice break from Melbourne in a part of the country I'd never seen—and maybe an opportunity to scout around for new customers in the regional towns on the way. Or so I thought. But then I heard about a run-down cottage for sale in Quaama for just $55,000 and my mind started ticking over. Even if a bank had agreed to take the risk of lending to me, the idea of using Dad's money to buy a sensible two-bedroom unit in Melbourne had never appealed. But here was a whole house, surrounded by abundant gardens, on a half-acre block. I could buy it without the need for a bank loan at all. Okay, it needed some repairs, and I arranged for the quotes: carpenter, plumber, electrician. I had the pest inspector come around—no problems. It was feasible. Back in Melbourne the following week, I rang Dad.

It wasn't what he'd had in mind, but he agreed to take a look. I continued with my due diligence and we met there three weeks later.

Dad walked through the house, tapping on walls, stomping on floorboards, emitting low whistles. Emerging into the sun, he sat down heavily on the end of the verandah. 'You know it needs massive repairs,' he said, frowning.

'Yes, and I've got the quotes.' I showed him my folder—jobs that I could pay for on my own income over a year.

He huffed and puffed; he wasn't happy. But he agreed to visit the agent and there he wrote a cheque for ten percent of the deposit—$550—the amount required to hold the property for ten days.

I was exultant. Over those weeks I'd invested much time and mental energy in this little tumbledown cottage and its wild grounds, this dilapidated slab hut with its uneven, gappy floors, its broken windows and non-existent plumbing. But more than that, I'd become attached. I was starting to feel, not that I owned it, but that it owned *me*.

That night I had an early dinner with Dad at the Cobargo pub, where he was staying, ten minutes up the road. Then I excused myself, bought a bottle of wine and drove out to Neehar's to celebrate with him and Nirda the purchase of the cottage and the beginning of my new life.

But the road ahead was a little bumpier than I'd imagined.

2. reduced circumstances

A week later Dad called to say he'd changed his mind. I was on a sales trip in Sydney. I was staying at Mum's place and had been very sick with the flu—in fact I was sweating and shivering in bed when he rang. I got dressed, dragged myself down to the car and was soon on his doorstep.

I had my folder of quotes for the repairs with me. When Dad answered the front door, I brandished it in his face. 'I've invested far too much time in this to let it go,' I said. 'You make a choice—keep your word or you'll never see me again.'

He hesitated, but only for a few seconds. 'No, I can't throw away good money on that house,' he said. I'd asked him to choose between his daughter and his money—and the money had won.

Don't start crying until you get to your room ... don't give him the pleasure.

Devastated, I returned to Mum's house. Since first seeing the house, I'd built a new, imaginary life there, and it was very hard to let it go. Mum met me at the door and saw my face. 'I didn't think he could hurt you anymore!' she cried. She'd never been happy that I'd rekindled a relationship with Dad.

But that afternoon, my grandfather rang. This was Dad's father; he and my mother had maintained a friendly relationship since the divorce. I answered the phone, and Grandpa asked me how I was.

'I feel like shit,' I said, and filled him in. He hadn't known about the house or Dad's offer. Then I called Mum to the phone and continued moping.

That evening, Grandpa rang back. 'I've been thinking,' he said. 'I want to lend you the money. But there's one condition: you don't tell your father.' I was elated, and of course I agreed. But in case you're wondering: yes, this is the same man who beat his wife and deserted his young family. That's what I'd heard. But I only knew him as a slightly distant old man with an ill-fitting toupée, who used to show up on Christmas Day with Mary, his 'dancing partner', and give each of us kids a five dollar note tucked into a charity card, and who lent me Tolstoy novels when I got older. By then he was politically socialist, if not communist (he was too rich), had visited Russia a few times, and had bought an office in central Sydney for People for Nuclear Disarmament when he heard that their landlord was giving them grief—Matt tells me there's a plaque there that recognises his contribution. Let's just say he'd mellowed.

The next morning I drove to Grandpa's house in Bexley, picked him up and took him to his bank. Upon hearing more about the house, Grandpa suggested that I borrow a little extra to help with the repairs. Within the space of twenty-four hours I'd gone from Dad's $50,000 loan with the promise of interference to a $70,000 loan and a whole lot more personal control. The next day I drove back down the coast, stopped at the real estate agent's office and paid the balance.

***

8 September 1997

Dear Jennifer,

I am printing this letter for the sake of clarity—my writing is deplorable.

When you were last here you asked me to write a statement regarding the term of my loan to you of $70,000 as my assistance to you in buying your home.

Sometime in July 1997 I took you to my bank and had the sum of $70,000.00 transferred to your bank account from my bank account.

I told you that I would not ask for interest to be paid to me on the loan but I would expect you to pay an interest of 2.5% to cover the deterioration of the dollar each year—that is in addition to the repayment of the principal in part (I might mention that interests vary from 7.5% to 15%).

In paying me 2.5% you are not causing me any monetary loss.

Best wishes.

Love, Grandpa

PS You might like to draw up a statement covering the acceptance of the money and the date thereof and post it to me. Grandpa

PPS To indicate monetary deterioration, when I was twenty-one I worked on the staff of the Goodyear Tyre Co. My wage was five pounds a week i.e. $10.00 a week, in those days a good wage. Today that wage would be $600.00 a week. Grandpa

* * *

One day stands out for me from that time. I couldn't have known it, but in retrospect it marks the last flare of Bhagwan's torch, the one I'd been burning from both ends.

It was September, 1997. I'd been in Sydney on another sales trip and on a Friday night had driven down to the Picton Skydiving Centre with my tent and sleeping bag to spend the weekend with Elise. A regular at the dropzone, Elise was scheduled to do her five hundredth jump, quite a milestone, and I was along for the party. I had no intention of doing a skydive myself, but I was looking forward to the celebrations.

The skydiving crowd was friendly and inclusive, but inherent in all their friendliness was a clear message: I wasn't a jumper so I would never really understand what life was all about. I didn't mind—they were a good bunch. All day Saturday I sat on the grass outside the clubhouse, watching trails of dots appear in the wake of the light plane high above, then form circles, spirals and stars before exploding into individual canopies and floating slowly earthwards. They'd glide to the ground and hit it running, or skidding, or rolling. But they'd always approach the clubhouse draped in their silky parachutes with mile-wide grins and eyes shining. 'Why don't you try it? Go on!' I'd smile and shake my head.

Towards the end of the day, Elise dropped into the sky for the five hundredth time. I couldn't make out exactly which black dot was her, but as the first jumpers of her load hit the ground and walked in, they were wide-eyed. 'Elise had a mal!' they told me. When Elise finally landed she explained that her main parachute had malfunctioned and she'd had to detach it, wait a few seconds, then open the reserve chute.

'You know the scariest thing?' she said. 'My heart rate didn't even go up. I've done it—I've used up all my adrenalin. What now?'

That night we were eating dinner at Picton's Chinese restaurant with a few of Elise's friends. We were drinking, we were laughing—about Elise's 'mal' among other things—and of course the talk turned to me and my reluctance to skydive. I scrabbled around for excuses, then hit on the one I was sure was a clincher: I simply couldn't afford the $400. There were nodding, sympathetic looks—after all, these guys were all stony broke. But at the other end of the table I noticed a whispered discussion involving the dropzone manager, Chris. Tandem master Mick, sitting beside him, nodded and they fell silent.

Pete, the cameraman, cleared his throat. 'We'll let you jump tandem, video and everything, for free, on one condition. You've gotta do it naked.'

'Naked jump! Naked jump! Naked jump!' the chant went up around the table. What could I say? I was drunk. I laughed and agreed.

Sunday morning dawned bright and crisp, as they tend to do when you're hung-over. It was early spring, the sky clear and blue. Overnight I'd prayed for rain to ground the plane, but the weather gods weren't on my side. I made my way to the clubhouse. I was booked on the nine o'clock load. In a daze of terror and self-recrimination, I signed the medical and legal release forms while Elise brought coffee and toasted sandwiches. She was elated. I couldn't, wouldn't let her down.

In a corner of the hangar I shucked off my clothes and allowed Mick to help me into the bulky harness. He'd decided to jump naked too, in the spirit of it. He found me some baggy shorts and a jumper to wear over the harness until we jumped—'After all, it's minus thirteen degrees up there,' he grinned. Over on the airstrip, we all piled into the plane. There were no seats—we sat in two columns on the metal floor of the cabin, each person straddling the one in front. Everyone else was kitted out in nylon jumpsuits, caps and boots.

Mick had explained to me exactly what would happen and I closed my eyes to go through my instructions one last time as the plane took off and gained altitude. Roll up when we jump, count to five, straighten up, bend knees, arms out in front. But really, all I could think was, either this will be the experience of a lifetime, or I'll die. One or the other.

Now we're at 13,000 feet and I'm pulling off my jumper and shorts, putting on goggles. There's happy excitement all around. Mick's clipping his harness to mine, from behind, and it feels like some kinky sex act. I'm achingly cold, but the shaking's got nothing to do with that.

People are rolling out the door. Just like that—they're in the opening, looking sideways, then they're gone. Now it's our turn. Mick takes my weight and I draw up my knees and hug them close. I look down. Nothing. Then we're tumbling, tumbling ... With each turn I catch a glimpse of patchwork green and ochre far below. The rush of air is deafening, and it's cold, the air so cold my throat closes around it ... I can't breathe but it doesn't matter, we're shooting down, across, swooping in an icy whoosh and nothing matters, nothing ever will again ...

The green and ochre patches are closer now and Mick taps me on the arm. There's a jerk and silence, pure, blue silence, as the torrent ceases. And now we're floating, wafting. The ground rises to meet us. I hug my knees again as Mick lands, jogs briefly and stops.

Word has got around the dropzone that a naked jump has landed so there's a crowd when I get back to the clubhouse. I'm draped modestly in yards and yards of parachute—Mick has made a run for it. The fabric shimmers in the bright sun and is gossamer silk against my skin; my bare feet savour the cool dew on the grass. A soft breeze works its way through the canopies of the gums around me and my heart leaps with the joy of it all.

Long Road to Dry River

* * *

If I'd waited just three months I wouldn't have been able to sign those medical waivers.

Back in Melbourne, my plan was to complete my list of renovations on the Quaama cottage and rent it out for a few years while I built up the wholesale jewellery business. But I was starting to experience strange sensations, a feeling of having tight bandages wrapped around my hips and knees. My legs felt weak and I was very tired. I was also getting tingling up my spine whenever I dropped my head forward. At first I thought I'd been overdoing it at the gym but when I took a break from working out the feelings remained. I visited an osteopath a few times but it didn't help.

One day I was in a café with my friend Jen Coleman, whom I'd met in 1991 when she was a dialysis nurse and I was working for Domedica. Now she was working with a neurologist specialising in multiple sclerosis at a major Melbourne public hospital. Over coffee I mentioned the tightness, the tingling.

Jen's face changed as she listened. 'I think you'd better see my boss,' she said.

I went cold.

A month later, in mid-December, I was sitting in the neurologist's consulting room as he placed my MRI scans on a lightbox and pointed out the handful of tiny bright spots that twinkled like stars in my brain and spinal cord. My surroundings seemed to have shifted an arm's length away; events were happening in slow motion; sounds had taken on an almost imperceptible echo.

'You have multiple sclerosis.'

The doctor may have gone into details but I wasn't really listening.

'Are you here alone?'

I suddenly felt very alone indeed. He advised me to go home, and, of all things, take a warm bath with some essential oils, and make another appointment to see him some time soon.

It was now clear that I'd had multiple sclerosis for ten years, since that night in the lecture theatre in Sydney when part of my field of vision had gone black.

Long Road to Dry River

The double vision of five years before completed the picture. And if I hadn't known it already, now I was sure—I needed to change my life radically. I needed to rethink my busy, challenging but, if I was honest, empty and unrewarding Melbourne existence.

I'd been reading a novel by Anne Tyler about a family living in 'reduced circumstances'. Maybe I'd missed the point, but something in that expression made my whole being sit up and say, *That's what I need—I need to reduce my circumstances!*

Lying there in the bath, in a fog of lavender and ylang ylang, I knew exactly what to do. I would start the renovations in Quaama and get out of the city as soon as possible.

* * *

I sounded very level-headed, didn't I, that afternoon in the bath? I felt very level-headed, with my practical plans and life-affirming decisions. But a week later …

I'm driving north along the Chandler Highway in Melbourne, heading home, crossing the bridge, the Yarra flowing muddily below. Everything's fine. I'm singing along with Chumbawamba on the radio. 'I get knocked down, but I get up again …' Then I'm sobbing—great, gulping, ragged sobs. I pull over and ring a friend, a kind Iranian man. I drive straight to his house, where he makes up the sofa, drops around to my place for some clothes and a toothbrush, and plies me with golden-crusted tahdig rice, fragrant eggplant stews and other Persian delicacies, holding my hand, stroking my hair and not saying anything much at all. After four soggy days I pull myself together, wipe my swollen eyes and launch my weary self towards a new future.

3. dry river

Jen Coleman gave me some information leaflets about multiple sclerosis—or MS as it's more commonly known. I took them home and left them in a pile on the kitchen table for a few days. There were photos of healthy-looking young people, some holding walking sticks or in wheelchairs—but smiling. The MS Society media unit had moved on from the Readathon posters of the early 1980s.

Eventually I started reading. MS is a disease of the nervous system. Damage to the nerve cells—initially, to the myelin, the fatty sheath that insulates the cells—causes the signals carried by those cells to slow down or go awry. Imagine a power cord with damage to its plastic coating. MS can cause visual problems, as I knew already. It commonly affects the legs, causing difficulties with walking, and less commonly the arms and hands. It can damage sensory nerves too, so people with MS often experience weird sensations—numbness, pins and needles, hot or cold 'patches' or pain. That explained that feeling of tightness around my hips and knees, and the tingling in my spine.

I turned back to the guy in a wheelchair, smiling at a girl propped on a stick, on the cover of the leaflet. I'd done a bit of bushwalking with Sukh in my 20s but had never really been keen on sport. Lately I'd settled into a pretty sedentary lifestyle with a token, weekly visit to the local gym. I liked to read and watch TV. I could imagine earning a living doing something sitting down.

So, as devastating as the diagnosis was, I tried to find the bright side. It wasn't terminal, and it didn't affect a sedentary person like me as much as it might affect an active, sporty person, or someone who depended on their physicality for their income—a professional skydiver, say, who would feel the diagnosis a lot more keenly.

I didn't choose that example lightly. Elise had rung me: Mick, my tandem master that day at the Picton dropzone, had been diagnosed with MS too. It was the end of his career, the end of life as he knew it. He'd left the dropzone and no-one knew where he'd gone.

***

I spent that Christmas in Sydney with Mum, Matt and Jon, and Jon's wife Flavienne, an exotic (to us, at the time) French woman he'd met in London. Jon and Flavienne were visiting from France and were expecting their first child.

I told Matt about the diagnosis. I'd been concerned that my long held resentments may have played a part. I encouraged him to try to break free of negative feelings and memories, but it wasn't clear to either of us how that might be achieved.

I didn't tell Mum about my MS that Christmas. I expected her to take the news badly and become very stressed. I hardly had the energy to look after myself, let alone to look after Mum too. I needed to get over this relapse before breaking the news to her; I wanted to be able to say, 'Mum, I've got MS but look at me, I'm fine'. I was lethargic and tired that Christmas. MS was causing me spells of overwhelming weariness, or 'fatigue', because my immune system was always producing and circulating cells and proteins that were supposed to be kept for fighting infections. These were telling my body to 'rest and recuperate', unnecessarily. But I explained away my tiredness at the time by saying I was on antibiotics for cystitis—Mum knew I had a history of such complaints.

Six months later, my legs were always sore and tired but the overwhelming fatigue that had dragged me down at Christmas had lifted, so that winter I decided to tell Mum. She took the news much better than I could have hoped and seemed to understand why I hadn't shared it with her before.

***

In the 1840s, when white settlers started squatting here, Quaama was a comfortable day's ride with bullock and cart from Bega, a well-established supply town about thirty-five kilometres south. It soon boasted a coach-house—with working girls, according to reliable sources; a general store for provisions; and a post office to service these businesses. All on the banks of Dry River—a river that ran underground for most of its length, most of the year.

In 1997, when I bought the cottage, Quaama still had its general store, which doubled as the post office, tripled as a two-pump fuel stop. There was a small but thriving primary school with three composite classes of spirited kids in blue shorts and red T-shirts—and both flags, Australian and Aboriginal, flapping proudly on poles at the gate. There was a School of Arts Hall, a small, weatherboard Anglican church and a central Anzac Memorial Park with a barbecue, swing set and slide. The village was surrounded by cattle country, mostly dairy—black and white Holstein Friesians—but with more and more glossy Black Angus beef cattle as the supermarkets pushed down the farm-gate price of milk ... but let's not go there.

I was quite taken with the explanation for the unusual name when I looked into it: apparently Quaama meant 'squabbling ground' in the local Djiringanj language—although this, you might have guessed, is itself disputed. Another translation offered was 'shallow water', which made sense—as I said, Dry River is mostly subterranean. Later, Djiringanj and Ngarigo man David Dixon told me about an ancestor of his, 'Koma', who was 'encountered in her natural state' by European colonists at Dry River in the 1830s (shortly before Quaama was first colonised and my house was built). Maybe I'm a romantic, but I love this first-contact image of a beautiful young woman bathing in the river, white men on horseback stumbling across her, shyness all around. The meeting is mentioned in anthropological recordings of South East NSW held in the South Australian Museum.

So I had shallow water, Koma and hints of minor disputes. Then I spoke with Sue Dickson. Sue worked with the Aboriginal Education Program at the Australian Catholic University in Sydney before retiring to the far south coast in 1999. Before she left work she mentioned to some colleagues, Yuin women, that she had bought a property near Quaama. They told her that she had chosen well, that Quaama had long been a meeting place for their forebears to conduct tribal business and sort out disagreements. In practical terms there was enough food, water and shelter to cater for the masses of people who would collect, but more, it was a powerful place, conducive to mediation, resolution and reconciliation.

Whether that's what 'Quaama' means is another thing entirely. But I like to sit on the riverbank, in my mind's eye families setting up camp beneath the eucalypts, deliberating around fires long into the night, leaving with bellies full and peace in their hearts.

* * *

As for my own block on Bermaguee Street, the age of the house made any renovations complicated. But I loved the history entrenched in it. The internal walls were built of thick hardwood slabs, set vertically. These slabs had adze marks, cuts where the swing of the horizontal axe had bitten, meaning it was built before 1850 when the Quaama sawmill had been established. This dated it to Quaama's earliest settler days. In my early, heady days of ownership and discovery, I removed some of the old pressed metal that lined a kitchen wall and found layers of draught-stopping newspaper dated 1939 glued over the slabs, with advertisements for hats and shoes priced in shillings and pence. To think that the house was already almost a century old by the time those earlier renovations were done. And one day after lifting floorboards the builder handed me three 1940s pennies he'd found. Eventually, I thought, I should do some research, find out about my predecessors. All I knew about was the family of Carmel Conway, who sold me the house, and a rumour of an old man decades earlier who died at the kitchen table. A dairy farmer down the road told me that the house had been derelict for some time in the 1960s, and he and his friends, as kids, had believed it haunted. They used to dare each other to run up the overgrown path and knock on the door.

The old six-inch floorboards, from before the days of tongue-and-groove, were polished with use and had wide draughty spaces between them. There was a big hole in the kitchen wall, tacked over with plywood and a sheet of flapping black plastic, where the fireplace and chimney had toppled down. Windows were missing panes of glass, and some panes still there were so old that the garden outside appeared in undulating waves.

There was no real bathroom—just a small area boarded off the verandah with a pale green, chipped enamel bathtub, a fast-recovery water heater and shower rose, and a big ceramic basin on a small chest of drawers, but no taps. And no toilet, just a 'long-drop' out the back—a deep hole in the ground over which a platform had been built with a rudimentary pan and seat, slab-walled on three sides (the fourth afforded a ruminative view over the back paddock). Carmel had been a tough old bird.

I can imagine you beginning to side with my father here. I do admit that there were times I'd retreat to the sofa on the verandah and cry at the size of the task I'd taken on. But they were tears of exhaustion, not regret.

There was no hot water in the kitchen. Carmel had boiled a kettle on her two-burner camp stove to wash the dishes. She left rows of empty preserving bottles on the shelves when she moved out, and string bags hung from hooks in the ceiling—to keep dry food from the mice, she'd explained. A short length of timber propped against the edge of the scratched, discoloured enamel sink was lettered in felt-tip, 'So the critters can escape'. Carmel had moved out a month before I took possession, and hadn't wanted lizards to get trapped in the sink (I imagined the poor things scrabbling at the sides until they starved and collapsed, and made sure I always left their little ramp in place when I went away).

In my first days in the cottage, I found magpies and king parrots lined up on the verandah railing, clearly expecting a feed. Small geckoes ventured in the back door and hung around, watching me. I threw them some crumbs.

Long Road to Dry River

* * *

Despite my expectations of the Hoffman Process I'd continued my run of inappropriate liaisons. I was passed like a pass-the-parcel at a children's party, one layer being peeled off every time the music stopped, and sometimes a trinket or two being revealed. Except I was a self-determining parcel. I dictated the layers, the trinkets, even the music.

In Melbourne, in 1995, I met Angus—tall, gangly, freckled—at a craft fair where I was exhibiting my handcrafted, original designs of silver and semi-precious stones. He was hawking 'ugly mugs'—rough-hewn pottery mugs with contorted faces on them. We started doing sales trips together, although we had few customers in common. I was dumbfounded at the orders he took—people wanted to drink out of those things? *That* many people?

Our relationship was tortured and dramatic, punctuated with painful break-ups and passionate reconciliations.

Gate Three, Indira Gandhi Airport, Delhi. I'm slouched in a plastic chair in grotty jeans and T-shirt, immersed in a paperback and recovering after the five-hour bus trip from Jaipur. Sporadic, unintelligible announcements in Hindi and English litter the air and the stink of

Delhi, the grit, the fumes, fill my head. I burrow into my book.

There's a tap on my knee.

'Madam?'

I look up. A sari-clad woman sits opposite. 'Madam? Someone is wanting your attention.' She gestures.

I look to my left, and there's a Rajput prince staring intently down at me. He wears a silk salwar kameez, an elegantly wrapped turban and leather slippers—the type that curl up at the toes. Under one arm he holds an enormous bunch of red roses, and in the other a shopping bag. He falls to one knee.

'Memsahib?' The accent is strangely Australian and reality slowly dawns. He's found me.

Angus was a stuntman. No, he didn't crash motorcycles for films or jump from speeding trains. He'd go for weeks, seemingly oblivious to my existence, then at the slightest hint I'd had enough he'd perform some amazing act of creative dare-devilry to prove his commitment. Once, he drove through the night from Taree on the north coast of New South Wales to Albury in the very south, searched hotel carparks for my car, and knocked at my door at 7 am—'Breakfast, madam!'—with a tray loaded with fresh fruit and champagne. I should have known—I hadn't ordered breakfast.

This time we'd agreed to separate, forever, in Delhi a week before. He'd gone east to explore the wilds of Uttar Pradesh. I'd gone west to lick my wounds with friends in Jaipur. I thought I'd been tricky, doubling back a week later to fly to Pune, but Angus had bribed an Indian Airlines official to search passenger lists for my name, and now here he was in a turban, with his roses and a last-minute ticket on my flight.

Now he's digging around in the shopping bag. He's brought out a small soapstone box inlaid with semi-precious stones, and he's opening it, and nestled in some tissue paper is a silver ring with a single glittering stone. 'Will you marry me?'

He's down on one knee on the scuffed linoleum, and my fellow passengers, I suddenly realise, have been soaking up this little scene. Their comments start to enter my consciousness.

'Where are the cameras?' one asks.

'Yes, they must be shooting a film!' responds another.

Some are leaning towards me, others behind have stood up for a better view. I feel the hot breath of a star-struck youth on my neck.

'Will you marry me?' asks Angus again.

'Um, yeah, OK.' It doesn't really matter what I say, as this is just a dream—isn't it?

That familiar grin spreads across Angus's face as my flight is called. I'm dimly aware of the gate lounge exploding into applause as I hear those further from the action asking their neighbours, 'Did she say yes? Where are the cameras?'

* * *

So Angus was young and fun and reckless ... until I brought him to Quaama in June 1997 to have a look at the rickety but charming cottage I was thinking of buying. I gave him 'The Tour', starry-eyed, detailing my plans: a sunny office here, a snug bedroom there, this corner room a bathroom, with a tub beneath a long, low sash window ...

'It's sick, Sahi.'

'OK, I did tell you it needs a bit of work—'

'A bit of work? *A bit of work?* It needs to be bull-dozed!'

I'd invested two years of my life in this man. How could he not see what I could see, what the cottage could become? This was the last straw—I drove Angus to the bus-stop in Bega the next day. The ring went into stock. I think I sold it to a New Age bookshop in Wollongong.

* * *

In 1998 I was travelling between Melbourne and Quaama on a regular basis to supervise the renovations. Robert ran the Big Nothing Café in Genoa, a small town on the highway just over the Victorian border. He'd named it in the spirit of the Australian penchant for big things—the Big Merino, the Big Banana, the Big Prawn ... When customers asked, 'So, where's the Big Nothing?' he'd point out the window at a distant hillside, empty except for a few sheep. They'd squint through the window, frowning.

Then I settled in Quaama. John was a fascinating narcissist with a middle-management job in Melbourne, ex-wife issues, and an unlimited mobile phone account, spelling many long, late-night conversations. It was, for extended but satisfactory stretches, a long-distance relationship.

John sometimes used Quaama as a bolt-hole. But I knew we were in trouble when he arrived, unannounced, at ten o'clock one wintery Tuesday night and admitted he'd told his line manager that he needed time off because his 'girlfriend with MS was having a crisis'. In fact, it was John who was having yet another crisis. I was indignant at being used. And he was amused at my indignation. How long had I been a convenient excuse?

A local guy followed that, the most inappropriate in my catalogue of inappropriate relationships, but providing me at last with the Grail—a few weeks of unencumbered, guilt-free, exuberant sex. Until one day in bed I told him I was approaching peak fertility, and to please be careful. But he looked me grimly in the eye and ... Later he would tell me that in that instant he saw the possibility of having me forever. But it was the end of our relations, unless you count lifts to and from Pambula Hospital, and his abject ministrations in the days that followed. Yes, I had an abortion. There. I said it.

4. an aged shearer in Rajasthani princess drag

That first year, 1999, I visited Quaama whenever I could get away. I'd taken possession of the cottage in summer, and as much as I'd enjoyed the long-drop toilet with its open view, the weather would cool. A girl's gotta have a bathroom—an indoor bathroom. But first the house had to be restumped, after which the floors were level but most of the doors either wouldn't budge or swung wildly, leaving a gap of an inch—or four—at the bottom or top. I had the house re-plumbed and rewired and eventually I removed a couple of internal walls to open up the space.

I engaged a local carpenter to pull up the floorboards and lay them back again flush. In each room he needed a couple of new boards to finish the floor, the old ones had shrunk so much (later a neighbour told me that Carmel hadn't minded the gaps—they were handy for draining the water when she hosed the house out). Then he installed a big window I'd found in a second-hand building supply store in Bega to fill the gap in the kitchen wall left when the fireplace and chimney had come down. There was a slow combustion stove to heat the house anyway, and now the room was a lot brighter.

The rain was torrential that first summer; drips and even rivulets appeared here and there inside the house. For days I moved buckets and saucepans around to catch the leaks and emptied them over the verandah. Huge blooms of mould flowered on the ceilings.

I'd kept my granny flat in Melbourne for a year and was getting contract work so I managed to tick off most of the major cottage renovations—the roof, the restumping and floors, the rewiring, the bathroom, and a long list of minor but essential repairs—before I moved to Quaama permanently. I came to know the Princes Highway very well as I drove from Melbourne to Quaama and back, usually with a trailer of furniture.

Each time I arrived back in Quaama, I was overwhelmed with a feeling of homecoming. I'd leap from the car and wander around the beautiful garden, noting a bulb shooting here, a new bud or flower there (and, yes, a dead plant here or there too, now that

Carmel and her attentions had gone). Whenever the house and its deficits felt too hard, the garden was a refuge—a chaos of flora, birds and insects, humming, buzzing—a scented realm of colour and life.

It was really the garden that had sold me—a wild, rambling cottage garden, with paths and nooks and secret corners. There were parts that I was still discovering months after I first took possession. I'd never had a garden and was a bit worried about its upkeep, but the wildness of the place attracted and reassured me—I could never have managed a manicured garden. I'd asked Carmel about its maintenance. 'Oh, I just pull out the weeds as they pop their heads up,' she soothed me with her Irish lilt, and I envisaged something I could achieve on a daily stroll, cup of coffee in hand. Of course, Carmel had been a full-time gardener. This garden had been her retreat and her sanity in the years since the loss of her husband and two of her sons. The three had died in the mid-eighties, all within eighteen months of each other. I often thought of my mother's words—how the only time her mind was quiet was in the garden. I magnified Mum's sadness a thousand times and imagined Carmel taking refuge from the infinite sorrow of those deaths, and seeding this wonderful, wild jungle of a garden from her losses.

Stan O'Donnell next door had worked in a commercial nursery in the late 1980s. He told me he'd bring dying plants home—shrubs, flowers, ferns, succulents, anything—'just pots of sticks', he said, and that Carmel would find a place, plant them, and nurture them. Imagine her relief—something she could bring back to life.

But a fulltime gardener I was not, never would be. It didn't take long for me to realise that a half-acre of garden, however unruly, was not something that could be maintained during my daily coffee-break, or even in a dedicated hour or two a week. When I first bought the place, Mum had come to visit with her sister, my Auntie Julie, and the two of them had run around the garden like children, giddy with delight, shrieking when they lost each other or themselves among the meandering paths and nooks in the hedges. After I made the final move in December 1998 Mum spent her regular visits—still timed for the school holidays even since retirement—on her knees weeding. We'd do an inspection together when she arrived and draw up a list of the most urgent garden jobs. She was happy to be helpful. Sometimes I'd help, pushing wheelbarrows of prunings and weeds to the compost, or to the fire heap in the back paddock.

But more often we'd just meet up for meals, or a coffee. I was glad to not have to talk, and I suspected that Mum was too. After a week, Mum would pack her bag into the boot of her tidy hatchback, and we'd tell each other what a lovely time we'd had.

Sometimes Mum brought Auntie Julie. The three of us would go to Cobargo or Tilba or Bermagui and have lunch or cups of tea. At home, Julie and I spent hours chatting on the verandah, occasionally spotting Mum's pale blue towelling hat bobbing around behind a hedge.

***

I'd continued to do occasional consulting work for Domedica and in April 1998 the CEO asked me to do a short job which involved a trip to the UK. I agreed readily: Jon and Flavienne, back in France, now had a baby—a son, Baptiste—and it would be a good opportunity to visit.

My suitcase was loaded with Mum's gifts for her first grandchild and I struggled to get it off the platform and onto the train at Paris's Gare Montparnasse. I was already exhausted, my legs aching, after a long search for the right platform, said suitcase in tow. And now I found myself in tears of frustration. I couldn't help casting murderous looks at people nearby, even railway staff, who were watching my difficulties with mild interest.

I made it to Amboise in the picturesque Loire Valley, where Jon and Flavienne had a house in a nearby village not much bigger than Quaama. Life centred on six-week-old Baptiste, of course, but one afternoon

Jon and I went for a walk up a hill nearby and, sitting down with the muddy pasturelands and smallholdings of the village before us, I told him of my diagnosis. He was concerned for me, of course, but he was a new father and soon the questions turned to heredity and genetic factors, something I hadn't even thought about. Later I was able to email him some figures that suggested that Baptiste was two or three times more likely than the average person to develop MS, due to his shared genetics with me. This sounded alarming, but it still meant a risk of only two or three in a thousand.

* * *

In those early days, MS mostly made itself felt below my waist. One minor but inconvenient exception first became apparent at the Quaama post office.

The post office was a counter at the back of the store. The postmaster had taken a dislike to me from my early days in the village. We'd had a minor dispute when I piled some of Mum's garden prunings in the paddock behind my back fence. My neighbour, Stan, had advised me to do so—'That's what everyone does'. But it turned out that the postmaster held the lease on that block, and I should have asked first.

'Please cease and desist!' he said, stonily, down the phone.

'Stan said the Fire Brigade can use the pile as an exercise during winter,' I countered—helpfully, I thought.

'I'm the Fire Chief!' he spluttered.

There's no mail delivery in the village—we have to collect mail from the post office counter. And from that day, the postmaster would hand me my mail, red-faced and grim, with a grunt. I had to admire his resolve, but after a few months I decided to get a post office box so I could access my mail from the shop porch.

One day there was a parcel notification, however, and I had to venture inside.

The postmaster pushed a small package across the counter, with a pen and a form. 'Sign, please.'

I took the pen, placed its tip where he indicated, and went to start a J. No response. I stared at the sheet of paper and tried again. He was waiting. Nothing, again. I breathed in, relaxed my arm, took a light but masterly grip on the biro … which shot out across the page.

The postmaster stared at my efforts, wordlessly. I put down the pen, mumbled some excuse and promised to be back for my parcel another time. And until that postmaster's retirement I picked up parcels on Wednesdays, his day off, when I would have no trouble at all producing a neat signature while chatting with his wife.

Years later my handwriting started to deteriorate into an uneven scrawl that even I had trouble deciphering at times. But in those early days this was new and only happened under duress. These days I joke with the new postmaster. After I explained my limitations, he told me that just an X in the box would be perfectly adequate. He knows who I am.

***

The other above-the-waist exception was more frightening.

I first became aware of what heat could do to me one afternoon at a 'sweat lodge' ceremony on a property just outside the village. Our host, Angela, had an affinity with Native American culture and had built a mud-brick dome a short distance from her house for such events. There was a flued cast-iron firebox in the dome, and Ange had been stoking it all day. When the dome was like an oven inside we all stripped naked and piled inside—there were about twenty of us, all women—and sat on low wooden benches on the mud floor.

The sweat lodge is a purification ritual in Native American culture. It's claimed that the scorching heat and the vapours from smouldering bundles of sage allow participants to attain a heightened perception or a connection with ancestors, or to gain access to new layers of self-knowledge. In our lodge that day, some women spoke in low tones of life challenges, some communed with their spiritual guides, some just sat quietly and sweated. Me? I went blind.

Well, not completely. Until Ange brought proceedings to a close I'd had my eyes shut so I hadn't been aware it was happening. When I opened them I found I could only make out blurry shapes of objects close to me, but enough so that when we all tumbled out into the cool evening air, I could find my way to where I'd left my robe, then follow everyone else back to the house, where I sat and drank herb tea and did my best to add to the chatter.

In MS, a rise in core body temperature can temporarily impair the ability of damaged nerves to conduct signals. Although I hadn't been experiencing visual problems—hadn't for years, since that double vision episode in Melbourne in 1994—my optic nerves must have been scarred.

That night at Ange's, I didn't let on to anyone that anything untoward had happened. I'm pretty sure I got away with it. I know what I was thinking—that as long as I pretended nothing was wrong, nothing was.

I waited at Ange's for a few hours, eating, drinking, chatting. By then my vision had cleared enough to drive home. It was only three kilometres along a quiet country lane, but it was a trip that took me a good ten minutes that night. I went to bed. By the next morning my eyes were back to normal, but I haven't so much as glanced at a hot tub since.

* * *

If I'd been at all concerned about this city-girl adapting to rural life, I was quickly assured. I loved life in Quaama.

Living in a small village fascinated and delighted me. I could walk around the whole of Quaama in half an hour—that is if I didn't get held up in a conversation, hailed from a verandah or stopped at the village store. Ros at the Quaama Store told me that I reminded her of Carmel Conway—it was the way I wore my hair. Everyone seemed to know who I was and where I lived. Everyone was interested in me, why I'd moved to Quaama, and what I intended to do now I was here. But soon I realised that everyone was interested in *everyone*. Quaama, I decided, was a smaller, hinterland version of Pearl Bay—the fictional coastal setting of *Seachange*, an ABC drama I'd been glued to weekly since early 1998. I and millions of other Australians were loving the alliances, friendships and romances, the bickering, rivalries and enmities that, apparently, were the everyday fare of life in a small town.

A friend told me, wryly, that in a small town it doesn't matter if you don't know what you're doing, because someone else always will.

I had wound down the wholesale jewellery business, finding the travel and the lugging around of kilograms of silver just too tiring. I had started taking on professional writing work. I was sure that I would soon be in a wheelchair and was determined to be able to support myself. Thanks to a contact in Melbourne, I started getting contracts for technical and commercial writing work with Telstra, Australia's major telcom.

Telstra paid well and I was able to get more jobs completed around the house. It would always be old and shabby but at least it was structurally sound, warm (enough) and comfortable. I carpeted over the remaining gaps in the floorboards and hung scarves and saris from my Indian travels over the rusty pressed metal wall linings ... a throw here, a cushion there ... think of an aged shearer in Rajasthani princess drag (kohl eyeliner, the works) and that was the old cottage by late 1999.

But after a year the Telstra jobs started to dry up; many of my contacts were leaving the company. So one day I sent my CV to the biggest employer in the area—the local cheese factory, a national brand. The next day their Human Resources Manager rang me.

'It says here that you recently completed a job for Telstra, a research paper, "How to Write for the Internet",' he said.

'Yes! Reading on-screen's very different from reading on paper, so content has to be presented differently—shorter words and sentences, using bullet points and other formatting devices—'

'Great!' he said. 'So, can you build us a website?'

I hesitated, but only for a second. 'Sure!'

I needed the work. How hard could it be? In Melbourne the following week I visited a technical bookshop and bought 'Learn HTML in 24 Hours'. I contacted the factory CEO's assistant and we agreed on site structure and content, and soon I had a few pages ready to show her. 'Go for it!' she said—and then it was live. My first website.

It didn't take me long to realise how bad it was. The front page was a lurid pasture-green with ten buttons—'About', 'History', 'Recipes', 'Contact Us', etc—around a sad-looking Holstein-Friesian cow, on whose side someone had artfully brushed a map of Australia. Site content was relevant and readable but a designer I was not. After a few months I offered to do a redesign, but everyone at the cheese factory loved their site and it was two years before they let me do a make-over, long after I'd removed the link to my business from the footer.

But many businesses were starting to see the advantages of 'an online presence' at that time and there weren't many other web designers on the Far South Coast. The business started to grow.

Long Road to Dry River

* * *

I was making lots of friends in Quaama and the surrounding area. One of the many advantages of sannyas is the instant community it confers. I've always found that wherever I've been in the world, I only needed to look up a sannyas commune or organisation, and soon I'd be swapping do-you-knows with someone. There'd never be more than two degrees of separation. Either we'd both been in Pune at the same time, or they'd worked on the Ranch in Oregon (the community set up around Bhagwan in the early 1980s) with a friend of mine … and it would go from there. I'm not going to say that all sannyasins like each other, or even necessarily share a world view, but there always seems to be a certain common level of understanding.

So when I arrived in Quaama I knew Neehar. And now I knew his sister Sangito, who lived ten minutes' walk away. Sangito had lived in Quaama, on and off, for thirty years. She had many friends. And many of her friends became my friends.

An added advantage of the far south coast sannyas community was, and is, its inclusivity—at any gathering there are plenty of non-sannyasins too. This isn't always the case—some sannyas communities can be quite exclusive. So I quickly met all sorts of people. The region is home to many creative types. There weren't many parts of New South Wales where you could buy a house, however decrepit, for $55,000—even in the late 1990s—in such a scenic locale. And those kinds of prices can be very attractive to creative people—those trying to survive on a writer's income, or an artist's, or a musician's.

At home, I loved it that people would visit unannounced—I'd come home sometimes to find a bag of leafy greens or the loan of a book on my kitchen table and quickly learned not to lock the doors (Mum was horrified).

I still felt that tightness around my hips and knees. If I was working in the garden, which I had come to love, I had to allow myself short recovery breaks throughout the day. This didn't worry me a lot. I'd just collapse on the lawn, surveying the fruits of my labour. I soon had two big, affectionate, playful dogs—ridgeback hound Harley in 2000 was joined a year later by his half-brother Gus—and they would flop down happily beside me, tongues lolling.

And every day I took the dogs walking, out the back gate and along a bush track to the Quaama Cemetery. At first I surveyed the grassy expanse, with three small clusters of graves at its perimeter, and thought it almost empty. But a chance encounter with the local gravedigger corrected that impression. Apparently the simple wooden markers used by generations of farming families had rotted away, so most of the graves were concealed. Rob explained to me his method of sinking a crowbar to distinguish between dug and undug earth and determine whether a plot was available, while we watched my dogs gallop joyful, sweeping circles across the field of unmarked graves.

I loved the cemetery, with its bushy surrounds, soft breezes and birdcalls in the canopy overhead. One day I chanced upon a scene there, and had to rush home to put the short piece it inspired on paper—an ode, I suppose, to Quaama Cemetery. I submitted it to the ABC and was invited to visit their Bega studio to record it so it could be broadcast for *Country Viewpoint*, a short segment at the end of the more newsy *Bush Telegraph*.

I had included a paragraph about the Conway graves:

> I always stop at three well-tended plots in a row on the river side of the grounds. Joe Conway and his sons Eamon and Brendan all died within eighteen months of each other in the mid-eighties. Eamon and Brendan were both in their twenties and died in motorcycle accidents. Their mother Carmel lived in my old cottage before me, and then moved to Bermagui, and the three graves are now adorned with seashells from her walks there as well as cheerful sprays of fresh and plastic flowers arranged across the trio of stone-edged plots. Since moving into the Conway cottage I have taken the liberty of claiming these men as my family too, and often stoop to clear debris from the graves as I walk past. I told Carmel; she doesn't mind. Around here they say that you're not a local until you have family in the cemetery, and so this is mine.

I bumped into Carmel in the supermarket a few days before the story was due to air, and told her that I had written about her family, the deaths, the graves, and that it would be on Radio National in a few days.

'Oh,' she said. '*Oh* …' She looked around us, then grasped my hand and hurried away. I wasn't sure if she was upset or just confused. I wondered if I should ring the ABC producer and pull the story.

But I let it go and trusted that all would be well. A few days after the story aired, Carmel rang me. 'I heard your story,' she said in that soft Irish lilt.

Heart in mouth, I waited.

'It was beautiful. I told Joe it was going to be on,'—Joe was her surviving son, in Queensland—'and he loved it too. He asked me to tell you that you're welcome to be a part of our family.'

5. other forces at play

One day in September 1999 I went to the post office to check my mail. There was a hand-addressed envelope and the writing was familiar. I turned it over: my Dad's return address. My stomach lurched.

My grandfather was now suffering early dementia and Dad had put him in a nursing home. I'd visited him whenever in Sydney, although it broke my heart each time. It was a very cheap facility—I suspect that Dad didn't want to spend too much of his inheritance. It reeked of urine and faeces overlaid with harsh disinfectant, and there always seemed to be someone screaming or moaning down the dim, linoleum corridor.

On one visit I noticed that Grandpa's fingernails had grown into claws, and I asked a nurse if I could borrow a pair of nail clippers. It took a long time for her to find some.

Once Grandpa was admitted, Dad had arranged power of attorney (jointly, with one of his sisters) over his father's affairs, and had gone through his finances. Grandpa couldn't prevent Dad finding out about the loan now. I could only imagine his shock and anger when he discovered what had happened. Dad had sent me a 'loan agreement' earlier that year, which I had, inadvisedly, signed and returned.

On the porch of the post office I unfolded this latest missive with trembling hands.

8 September 1999

Dear Jennifer,

Re: Loan from [AJH] - $70,000

As you are aware, your grandfather is now in a nursing home in Manly Vale following a recent illness which hospitalised him in May. Due to his failing health, he has appointed us his attorneys. In this capacity we are obliged legally to look after his personal and financial affairs.

According to your last payment on 20 April 1999, interest on the loan is outstanding for the period from May to August inclusive. We appreciate that due to circumstances you were probably unsure of how to deal with your obligations in this regard and would ask that you now bring your interest payments up to date by sending a cheque in the name of [AJH] to [my father] at the above address. These funds will, of course, be banked into the account of [AJH] and a receipt will be sent to you.

We trust that this letter finds you well and we look forward to receiving your payment.

Regards.

The letter was signed by both my father and my aunt.

I'd explained my difficulties to Grandpa when I received the MS diagnosis just months after he lent me the money, when I was experiencing bouts of fatigue. His response had been, 'Just do what you can, dear'. But clearly I couldn't expect the same leniency from my father and aunt.

I deposited $875.00 into Grandpa's account, but knew I hadn't heard the last of it.

The next letter arrived on 12 January 2001.

Dear Jennifer,

Repayment of loan

We are in the process of getting our father's affairs in order. According to his records he gave you a loan of $70,000 on 14 July 1997. Interest at the rate of 3% per annum was to be paid on the outstanding balance.

The total outstanding as at 14 January 2001 is $75,350. This is represented as follows …

Dad detailed the initial amount borrowed, the amount owing after interest and some of the repayments I'd made, calculating an amount of $75,350 owing. 'Would you please send a cheque for this outstanding amount to the following address within 28 days from the date of this letter.'

I had the stubs of my deposit slips. I'd made several payments that they'd missed; they'd made no mention of the $875.00. And they'd raised the interest rate by half a percent with no explanation. But those details paled beside their request for the whole amount—principal plus interest. I would have to sell the cottage. A friend suggested that I consult a lawyer, and that's where I was, down the peninsula from Melbourne, later in January 2001.

* * *

'Have you ever considered you might have got the MS because you can't forgive your dad?'

It would have made for an interesting conversation, but not in this stuffy office, and not with my solicitor. I quickly steered the conversation back to what legal means there were to hold my father and aunt at bay. The solicitor's advice that day mostly concerned the 'loan agreement' that Dad had sent me in early 1999, when he and Glennie had first learned of the arrangement. The agreement included a clause saying that 'the principal amount is payable on demand'. Later I was to berate myself for signing it without getting legal advice, but the doctor had advised me to avoid stress, and I'd taken the easy option. I couldn't imagine Grandpa demanding the principal back any time soon. He'd been very generous, and I didn't want to upset him by questioning the document. And I wasn't thinking ahead to a time when he wasn't in charge of his own affairs. But Dad was certainly thinking ahead—he saw a third of Grandpa's assets as simply a term deposit in his name.

The solicitor pointed out that the time for questioning the loan agreement had been before I signed it. I could hardly disagree. But he seemed to think that I might have a case in that the loan agreement which Dad and Glennie had written up differed from my original agreement with Grandpa. For a start, they had raised the interest rate. And of course there was the new clause about the loan being repayable on demand. As the solicitor said, it didn't make sense that a loan advanced for the purpose of buying a property should be payable on demand. I returned to Quaama to consider the solicitor's advice. But before we'd even responded, another letter arrived. Dad had engaged a solicitor too.

> We advise we are the solicitors for your grandfather [AJH] by whose Attorneys we have been instructed in relation to the loan of $70,000.00 made by him to you

> as evidenced by the Loan Agreement dated 26th July, 1997 ... The loan is repayable on demand ... unless satisfactory arrangements are made for the repayment of the loan within fourteen (14) days from the date of this letter then appropriate action to secure the recovery of the debt will be taken without further notice to you ...

I was trying to remain calm. I'd learned *pranayama*, a type of yogic breathing, at a weekend workshop in Melbourne before I'd moved, and I dug out the instruction manual. Every afternoon I would settle myself on a cushion on the rug in my lounge room and close my eyes. I would visualise each breath sequentially entering nine separate 'compartments' in my lungs, one by one, then gradually flowing out again. I'd progressed to the stage where I was only taking two breaths a minute. Then after half an hour of that I would sit in silence, still aware of the rise and fall of my belly, no longer counting the seconds, not really thinking about anything—until it got chilly and I rose to light a fire.

My solicitor sent an email to Dad's solicitor questioning the clause about repayment on demand and the new interest rate and asking for more time for me to consider my actions. The next letter arrived a month later. No mention was made of our questions. Instead, the demand for repayment and the threat of legal action were repeated.

Again my solicitor rallied. But there were no further letters from Sydney. Perhaps Dad and Glennie had decided to bide their time, knowing that Grandpa wasn't well and it would soon be within their power to make the full claim upon their inheritance.

***

In mid-2000 I'd discovered a book called *Taking Control of Multiple Sclerosis* by an Australian doctor, George Jelinek. Jelinek held the Chair of Emergency Medicine at Charles Gairdner Hospital in Perth. And he had MS.

Jelinek recommended a diet low in saturated fats and high in omega-3 fatty acids, maintaining high serum vitamin D levels, moderate amounts of exercise, and daily meditation. So far, so good. I'd been on a vegetarian diet since I first left home. So now I just had to give up dairy, not a huge sacrifice, and start eating fish—I could manage that too—and I was covered. I have the kind of skin that burns quickly in the sun and had always covered up, but I could supplement with vitamin D capsules. Exercise, well ... surely maintaining my half acre of garden, and long, rambling walks with my young ridgeback hounds was enough? And meditation—at that stage I had the *pranayama* and I was practising fairly regularly.

But I wasn't going to find the next part of Jelinek's regimen easy. It involved sorting out any old resentments and internal conflicts, in order to rid them from my life and be at peace. Jelinek was a strong proponent of the mind-body connection, and by now even the most conservative doctors agreed that stress could cause physical illness. But could I find inner peace as an adult without coming to terms with my past?

Any inner peace I'd attained after completing the Hoffman Process was much diminished after my father's withdrawal of his loan in 1997 and our acrimonious parting. And now, receiving his letters of demand, I'll admit to having feelings of resentment. He was a rich man, after all, and all I had was my house ... After each letter I'd retreat inside with a bout of neuralgia (nerve pain). Despite my attempts at Buddhist *metta bhavana* meditation—sending thoughts of 'loving kindness' to Dad—I was finding it hard to maintain my equanimity.

* * *

Early on the morning of 29 June 2002, the phone rang. It was Mum. Grandpa had died 'peacefully' in the night, or as peacefully as was possible in that facility, and the funeral was to be held the following week. Although it wouldn't make any difference to Grandpa, I wanted to be there.

As the day of the funeral approached, my neuralgia arrived in crippling form. I was unable to drive the distance so I flew to Sydney. The service, at the

Northern Suburbs Crematorium, was attended by perhaps twenty mourners, all family except a couple of representatives from People for Nuclear Disarmament, which was appreciated. I was momentarily stunned when Dad's sister Glennie came up and kissed me on the cheek. Dad didn't approach me, and I avoided him, but I knew that this was what he'd been waiting for.

16 August 2002

Dear Ms Severn,

RE: ESTATE OF THE LATE [AJH]
<u>LOAN TO YOU</u>

As you are aware by a letter dated 5th March, 2001 a demand was made on you to forthwith repay both the principal and interest on the loan.

Your grandfather now having passed away are [sic] in the process of finalising the Estate and the executors of the Estate require you to forthwith make arrangements for repayment of the full amount of the principal and interest and in that regard I look forward to receiving particulars of the arrangements you will put in place for repayment of the loan forthwith.

Yours faithfully […]

I was reluctant to drag the matter out any longer, recognising the physical effects that the stress was playing out on me. In any case, there were other forces at play, and in my favour.

Upon my grandfather's death, my father's other sister, Pauline, became involved. She was living in New York and had been unaware of Dad's and Glennie's activities with regard to their father's affairs. Pauline was a nurse, and when she learned of the demands they'd been placing on me she was horrified. She immediately told me that she would 'forgive' her portion of the debt, so that reduced it by one third. She also told me not to pay anything yet, to wait until I heard back from her.

It was six months of trying to stay calm, trying to just get on with my life.

But I was stunned when the next letter arrived, and not just at the new, conciliatory tone.

5 February 2003

Dear Ms Severn,

I have been instructed to confirm that both [Dad] and [Pauline] who are two (2) of the three (3) main beneficiaries of the Estate have agreed to relinquish their one third entitlement to the balance of the loan required to be paid by you.

Would you please make arrangements to repay one third of the outstanding balance to us by way of cheque made in favour of the Estate of the Late [AJH] within the next fourteen (14) days.

Should you wish to make some different arrangements or should you be unable to pay the funds within the time specified above then would you kindly contact the writer to negotiate a period of time acceptable to the Estate.

Yours faithfully [...]

I rang Pauline. She told me that, for her, the time for civilities was over. She'd threatened my father with legal action over an unrelated matter unless he also forgave his share. He'd folded—if Pauline had sued, it would make Dad's share of my loan look like loose change. Now I only owed Glennie. My mother sent me $10,000 and I borrowed the balance, some from Matt, the rest on credit cards. At last the whole sorry affair was over—I owned my house, outright.

Six months later I learned that my two brothers and six cousins had each received $12,500 from my grandfather's estate. My father had arranged for me to be excluded from the inheritance.

* * *

In early 2004 Jon called me. It started with the usual enquiries about my health, and general family news, but soon he got to the point, and he sounded a bit sheepish.

'The thing is, Jen, Dad has offered to lend us the money to buy a house.'

Jon had moved back from France in 2002 with Flavienne. By then they had two sons—Baptiste, and

Sébastien who'd been born in 2000—and had decided they wanted to bring them up in Australia. They were renting a house in Sydney's inner west, a situation that troubled Dad, of course.

The irony didn't escape me. But Dad's relationship with Jon had always been, if not fatherly, at least quite benign. I wondered if being a grandfather had stirred some new feelings in him—no grandchildren of his were going to be brought up in rental accommodation! And Jon, as reluctant as me back in 1996 to accept a loan from Dad, now had a family to consider. He and Flavienne were determined that she would be home for the children while they were young, and living in Sydney on a single income was hard.

'He's laid out a pretty generous repayment plan,' said Jon. 'The mortgage payments are going to be lower than the rent we've been paying.'

So, after a moment or two, I gave a wry chuckle. The house they were buying, although far from luxurious by Sydney standards, was valued at ten times the amount that Dad had hounded me for just a few years before.

'I'm really pleased for you,' I told my brother. And I meant it.

6. like a precious jewel

I was following George Jelinek's diet and my MS did not appear to be progressing. When I told my neurologist about the diet, he was not impressed. He said, 'Well, at least as you become more disabled you'll still be healthy on the inside'. Asking around, I learned that this was typical of neurologists' attitudes at the time. George Jelinek was an emergency specialist, not a neurologist, and maybe they resented his trespassing onto their 'patch'. Even so, I felt happy and optimistic about my management strategy. But when stressful circumstances reappeared in my life, I found that once again I was unable to deal with them.

In February 2006 I was on the last day of a writing retreat at Petrea King's Quest for Life Centre in the Southern Highlands. The receptionist came to find me during the morning break; my aunt had been trying to call me. I took my mobile to the carpark to try to get a signal. At last I got a scratchy connection, and Julie didn't waste time.

'I think you should come to Sydney, Jen. Your mum's a very sick lady.'

It was a call that I knew would come one day. Mum had been diagnosed with bladder cancer early in 2005, and had undergone surgery to remove the tumour. The doctor had used the word 'aggressive' at the time, and Mum had lost not only her bladder, but her uterus and part of her lower intestine as well. They'd removed some lymph nodes to check if the cancer was spreading. It was.

I'd spent three weeks in Sydney with her after that operation. Mum had to wear a plastic urostomy bag under her clothes to collect urine. PVC tubing connected it to an adhesive patch over an opening in her abdomen. It was hard to watch her coming to terms with the workings of her reconstructed body but she slowly came to accept this new existence and had started living her life again—gardening, tutoring a former student for his Higher School Certificate, even aqua-aerobics at the local pool.

Not long after returning to Quaama from nursing Mum in 2005, I was also diagnosed with cancer—melanoma. I was lucky, though. It was only Grade 1, or borderline Grade 2. I had the mole removed with a few lymph nodes for testing, and after ten tense days of waiting the results came though: all clear.

But underlying Mum's health issues and my own was a situation which made things even harder.

Just before Grandpa died in 2002 I'd met James, an artist who lived in the nearby coastal town of Bermagui. We were spending our weekends together, alternating between Quaama and Bermagui. Quaama meant a quiet, lazy weekend (well, James might mow the lawn), and a quiet dinner with friends. Bermagui offered Saturday brunch at a café, a dinner party with James cooking, and musician, writer and artist friends around the table in his artisan-built house until the early hours. The house was on a few acres at the edge of the Bermagui State Forest, just above Jaggers Bay on the Bermagui River. We woke each morning to the chime of bellbirds. Harley and Gus rambled happily over the property with James's young retriever Jack, and in the afternoons I loaded them into the back of my four-wheel-drive ute and gave them a run at the always-deserted Barragoot Beach, south of Bermagui, just for the joy of seeing them gallop along the tide line. If there wasn't a dinner party there was an evening on the verandah, chatting, sipping red wine and listening to the Wonga pigeons whooping across the valley as night fell.

Moving between Quaama and Bermagui suited us both, although we did start spending more weekends in Bermagui and fewer in Quaama as time went on. And James's emotional support was central to me when Grandpa died and for the harrowing six months until my debt was resolved, even if I'd had to recount the whole sorry saga to him over a bottle of red, one long evening early—too early—in our relationship.

But there were difficulties, incompatibilities. Despite relations between us becoming strained, James and I decided to take a trip to Greece in October 2005 to visit Hydra, an island he'd lived on briefly in his youth. Hydra was lovely. It rose steeply from the Mediterranean, a maze of cobblestoned roads too narrow for cars—the only mode of transport was donkeys. I enjoyed James's old friends; I relished the food—the simple but tasty seafood and vegetable dishes meant I could easily comply with my Jelinek diet; I revelled in the cultural history—a number of expat authors and musicians (Charmian Clift, George Johnston, Leonard Cohen) had colonised the island in the early 1960s. But the constant, enforced walking exhausted me and I missed my dogs sorely. And my relationship with James was deteriorating; as our return date drew near the tension became unbearable. I needed a break and caught the ferry to Mykonos to visit my old friend from Stricklandstrasse and our harbour flat at Parsley Bay—Swarna, who'd just had a baby.

A few weeks after James and I returned from Greece, we parted.

So that was 2005. Mum's cancer and my melanoma, relationship tension in the background, a difficult month overseas, the end of the relationship. And now, in early 2006, it looked like Mum's cancer was terminal. I left the Quest for Life Centre, drove home to pick up my dogs and some clean clothes, and departed again for Sydney.

Although Matt still lived with Mum, he was working and had many commitments at night. I realised how much of the strain Auntie Julie had taken on. I was there for five exhausting weeks before Mum died and it might sound strange, but it was one of the loveliest times of my life. I spent most of my waking hours looking after Mum's needs—helping her wash and dress, driving her to radiotherapy appointments (it was generally recognised that this treatment was palliative, for pain relief), coaxing her to eat and drink, and making sure she took her medications. The family was being caring and soft and gentle with each other.

Mum was desperate to live. She wanted to watch her grandchildren grow up. Even as she wasted away she spoke of her next round of chemo—'as soon as I'm strong enough'. It was clear to everyone else that she was dying, but no-one wanted to burst her fragile bubble. One day I realised how dehydrated she was and suggested we visit the hospital for an infusion of fluids. I helped her to dress and got her into the car. As I backed down the driveway I wondered if this would be the last time she saw her beloved home. It was.

Mum spent her final week at Manly Hospital, where she had her own room, and most nights there were three or four of us, sleeping on recliner chairs and spare mattresses, keeping watch over her as she slipped away. Mum had loved cryptic crosswords—it was a pastime that the whole family shared—and Matt had bought a couple of books of puzzles for anyone there to amuse themselves with. There was much hilarity as we struggled with the clues, too tired to think straight. If Mum was aware of her surroundings at all—and the nurses said she would be—she was enjoying it.

On 5 April 2006, as the midday Angelus pealed out from the bell tower beneath her window, we realised that Mum had taken her last stertorous breath. Her breathing had been erratic, with long pauses, so I had been wondering how we would know when the end had come. But it was as clear as this: one moment there were four people in the room, the next there were three.

I glanced up and saw Mum's teaching friend Maureen, on a chair against the wall, press her hands together under her chin, like a child. *Now I lay me down to sleep, I pray the Lord my soul to keep ...*

Long Road to Dry River

* * *

At the funeral the following week, as Matt and I walked along the footpath towards St Paul's, a white sedan pulled into the carpark.

'There's Dad,' said Matt.

I stumbled immediately and needed to lean on Matt's arm to get up the church steps. This was my first experience of an effect I have since become very familiar with—a sudden stressful situation can affect my balance and coordination from one step to the next. There's no physiological reason, with my MS at least, for this. It's to do with my state of mind.

But I couldn't fool myself that this general deterioration in mobility was just a state of mind; a year of relentless stress had taken my MS to the next stage. I now needed a walking aid.

* * *

After the funeral I returned to Quaama and started catching up with my work. For the first time I congratulated myself on my foresight. I couldn't walk straight but I could sit down at a computer.

I could still walk unaided around the house. I felt quite confident in the garden, and even walking around Quaama, or around the Quaama cemetery—

the dogs' favourite destination, where they'd race into the remnant bush at the perimeter, flushing out rabbits to chase. In fact, I found walking on soft ground—grass or bushland or paddocks—to be relatively easy. It felt like my feet were receiving signals, helping my balance and co-ordination.

But the pavements of Bega, where I did my weekly shopping, caused me great difficulty. I became quite self-conscious, aware that my troubled gait might make me look drunk. So it was perhaps my vanity, chiefly, that saw me in the pharmacy one day with my friend Hansa, trying out walking sticks. If vanity was a driving force then it also raised its head when I left the pharmacy that day and turned onto Carp Street with my new stick. I was sure everyone was staring. But the first two people we passed were both on walking sticks, then the third person was a cool, young, blonde woman, dressed in faded denim jeans and jacket, leaning jauntily on a stick as she chatted with two equally cool young women on the corner outside the bank. In that moment, my stick became a fashion accessory.

In practical terms, I recognised that the stick gave me an extra point of reference. I was now as sturdy as a three-legged stool. Still, I didn't need my stick inside, or around the garden. I just used it when I went out.

It's 2001 and I'm crossing Church Street in Bega, striding out across the old cobblestone gutter and onto the blacktop in my jeans and shirt and RM Williams boots, feeling sturdy and strong. I think, 'One day I'll remember this'.

'Walking, walking, walking,' I tell myself. 'Just walking.'

Now it's 2006. As I step out to cross Church Street, the cobblestones have become a trap for my stick and the blacktop an expanse to be covered one unsteady step at a time. But I hold that memory like a precious jewel. 'Walking, walking, walking. Just walking'.

* * *

I think it was also that day, the day I bought my stick, that I started to see Hansa as more than just a friend.

Hansa was—is—a local glass artisan. We'd known each other for eight years—since I moved to Quaama. I had first noticed him in 1998. He dropped by Sangito's house while I was visiting one day, very early on—a tall, quiet, bearded man in loose clothes. He slipped, elusively, through the back door and put a cassette tape on the kitchen counter, gave us a wave and left.

Sangito and I were in the lounge room. I turned to her. 'Who was *that*?'

She laughed. 'That was PH—Paramhansa. He was just returning a tape he borrowed. Sahi, *he has a girlfriend.*'

Was I that transparent?

So I'd always found him very attractive, even when I realised he was twenty years older than me. But he was in a relationship with Dasha, a lovely Czech woman, and I'd assumed they were happy—even if Dasha seemed to spend most of her time in either Sydney or Prague. But in 2005 they had quietly, formally separated. Not that I or any of our friends in Quaama had known of it, despite getting together for regular 'coffee mornings'. Now, in 2006, I was single, and Hansa made his feelings known. And I found how easy it could be to fall *in* love with someone I'd always loved.

Maybe it was because Hansa had been there at that critical time when my MS progressed that I've never since felt that I had to pretend to be stronger or more able or more energetic than I am. He knows what to watch for, and when I start to tire he just takes over. Just as I needed more help, the perfect partner arrived in my life.

* * *

At my next visit to my neurologist in Melbourne, he did a full examination then retreated behind his desk.

'You now have secondary progressive MS,' he said.

Most people with MS start out with a form called 'relapsing-remitting'. It's characterised by episodes of disability—'relapses', with visual or mobility issues, or sensory symptoms—that resolve over a few weeks, such as my attack of double vision in 1994. Then a period of 'remission' follows, where the person can experience normal health, or close to normal but with some minor left-over reminders of the relapse. It's possible to remain in this relapsing-remitting disease state for the rest of your life, but about two thirds of people eventually move on to 'secondary progressive' MS.

So, nineteen years after my first symptoms, it meant that my condition had become neurodegenerative—not just the nerve sheath, the myelin insulation, was suffering damage, but the nerve fibres themselves. And whereas the myelin usually underwent repair to some degree, the nerve damage was, to scientific knowledge at the time, permanent.

I knew about MS progression. But the news was still a shock. The specialist silently slid a tissue box across his desk. He was a man of few words.

In a fit of remorse, I asked, 'Did I make a huge mistake, turning down the drugs when I was first diagnosed?'

In 1998 this neurologist had been very keen for me to try Avonex, an interferon therapy, and at one stage I'd agreed. The starter kit arrived from the manufacturer, a small black canvas case complete with a multilayered sponge that simulated human skin, subcutaneous fat and underlying muscle, and a pack of hypodermic needles so I could practise plunging the needles to just the right depth before starting on my own belly, thighs and buttocks with the real drug. I would have to inject myself every second day. The pamphlets described flu-like symptoms too. After tossing a couple of needles, like close-range darts, at the sponge I stuffed all the contents back in the bag and zipped it up. It radiated fear, guilt and denial at me from the corner of my bedroom until I rang the doctor, opting out, and took it to the tip.

Now, in 2006, he sighed. 'As far as we can tell, if you'd started on an interferon therapy then, you might have delayed this outcome for a couple more years.'

Eight years of injections and flu-like side effects to delay my progression for just two years? That made me feel a bit better.

* * *

It was around this time that I got another call from my brother Jonathan. Just three months after our mother's death, he was being investigated for back pain and a scan had revealed a large tumour in his abdomen. Baptiste and Sébastien were eight and six, and they now had a little sister, Emeline, who was eighteen months old.

After two surgical procedures the doctors declared the cancer gone. They saw no need for follow-up chemotherapy or radiotherapy, and we all celebrated what we saw as a lucky escape.

In 2013 Jon would start experiencing pain in his abdomen again. He had another scan; despite his doctors' confidence after his surgery in 2007 his cancer had returned. There was a new, experimental therapy available now, involving infusions of a radio-isotope, and he was accepted onto the trial. Once again the doctors spoke in optimistic terms. Even if it wasn't a cure, we felt assured that this treatment would, at least, extend Jon's life.

* * *

Later in 2006 I got to know Liz Stenhouse, who had MS and lived near Tilba, about fifty kilometres north of Quaama. Liz had also been following George Jelinek's regimen for a few years, and we met to compare notes. A former high school science teacher, Liz had thoroughly researched complementary therapies for MS and shared many of her findings with me. She was also a regular attendee at a small private gym in nearby Narooma, and recommended that I make an appointment to see Jaimey Costin, the owner and instructor there.

Driving up to Narooma to meet Jaimey, I had visions of my old gym in Ivanhoe, the one I was attending at the time I was diagnosed in Melbourne. The Ivanhoe gym was one huge floor of rowing machines, treadmills, stationary bikes and weightlifting apparatus. The clientele varied but in my T-shirts and shorts I often felt a little under-dressed. And everyone appeared to be moving through their routines in isolation. In all my time there I can't remember ever having a conversation with another person, let alone making a friend.

So Costin's Gymnasium in Narooma was a surprise. Jaimey had converted the front three rooms of his cottage, had reinforced the floors, and had artfully arranged the bare minimum of equipment—one rowing machine, a couple of exercise bikes, some boxing equipment, a couple of benches and some free weights, dumbbells and bodybuilding equipment—in the limited space. As I answered Jaimey's questions and he started to work out a plan for me, I looked around the small area and the six people who seemed to be happily sharing it that day, each armed with a program on a clipboard (and, mostly, an attendant pair of reading glasses, it must be said). There was constant friendly banter as people moved from workout bench to rowing machine to floor mat, and not a stitch of Lycra to be seen. Jaimey allocated me a regular Tuesday morning session and I drove back home, already looking forward to starting my program.

Jaimey was far from the musclebound sports jock I'd imagined. He was fit and healthy, for sure, and looked at least a decade younger than his forty-seven years. But he'd studied Sports Science at the Australian Institute of Sport and had a long list of clients with MS—he was well-qualified to devise a program for me. In those early days I started sharing that Tuesday session with Liz and Bruce, who also had MS. I quickly became friends with them both and soon we were meeting for coffee after our gym sessions. Soon we were joined by Jenn, Fiona and Cecilia, three others with MS. Anyone with MS within cooee of Narooma and with any degree of self-preservation quickly finds their way to Costin's Gymnasium.

There are many types of intelligence and Jaimey seemed to have a high level of 'physical intelligence'. He could watch my gait and instantly know which muscles needed strengthening or stretching, and which exercises would best benefit me. In the same way, he prescribed exercises that improved my balance and my proprioception—the sense of knowing where your limbs are in space, even with your eyes closed. Although Jaimey and I tweaked this program over the years in line with my changing needs and new findings in MS research, it remained the basis of my Tuesday morning appointment for eleven years.

***

Mum left me some money in her will, and in 2007 I started to think about extending and renovating the old cottage. But as the quotes came in I realised that any builder asked to work on such an old building would, quite sensibly, quote worst-case-scenario prices because they just couldn't be sure of what they would find, once the work started. I'd learned that lesson in 1998—just putting a window in that hole in the kitchen wall left by the collapsed fireplace exposed rotting joists that necessitated earthworks to create airflow under the house, and the replacement of yet more floorboards ... and weatherboards ...

I made some enquiries and found that building a whole new house would not cost much more than patching up the old one. And since the block was a large one, I could have a new house up the back without losing the old cottage—a relief, as I would have been heartbroken to see the old place knocked down.

So with the help of a local designer, Hansa and I put a development application in to council in October 2007, and on a sunny day seven months later we moved into our new home, a solar-passive bungalow clad in grey-blue Colorbond steel. It was only twenty metres from the old cottage and a dozen friends came around that day to carry furniture, armfuls of clothes, and boxes of books, pots, pans and more up the path to the new house. After a couple of hours we were all set up.

Where the old house had been draughty and dusty, the new one was well-sealed. In the old house the bathroom was one step up, as was the verandah, which was on footings that hadn't sunk with the main structure. But the new house was all on one level—much easier to get around and important if there was any chance of needing to roll in, out and around in the future. Whereas the temperature in the old house pretty much tracked that outdoors, the new house maintained a steady internal temperature and was easy to heat and cool. There were two bathrooms, one off the bedroom and a guest bathroom at the other end of the house. Now that my bladder was becoming an issue for me (more on that later), not only could I usually be assured of a toilet being free at any time, there was always one close at hand.

The old cottage became Hansa's studio and turned out to be perfect for his work as a glass artist. My old light-filled office became his workroom, and the sunroom a small gallery. And who would have thought that the verandah would make such a perfect loading dock? Later he even converted the bedroom into a garage for his red Fiat Spider, removing the floor so he could drive straight in. He used the floorboards to build big, barn-style garage doors.

That first night in bed in the new house I was surprised to hear a familiar sound: a tiny bat flying laps of the room, a silky scissor-snip in my ear with each pass. The bat had been a tenant of the old house the last few winters. How, and why, had it moved into the new house? Then I realised—it must have been asleep between some clothes on my rack when a friend draped a bunch of hangers over her arm, carried them up the path and hung them in our new built-in wardrobe. We ushered it out the door, where, I hope, it found its way back into the old house to resume its nightly hunt.

7. get me to the porcelain

For nearly two more years, Hansa and the dogs and I lived happily in Bermaguee Street.

Then, in March 2010, Gus was diagnosed with bone cancer. He'd been in pain, favouring one hind leg when walking, and I thought he might have damaged a ligament, but the x-rays showed something much more sinister. I took him home but I knew what we needed to do, and soon: three days later I asked the vet to come to the house, and we all cried as she put him to sleep. He was only nine. I watched my stress levels at the time but because it all happened quite fast, and because the decision was clear, there was just simple, clean grief to deal with.

Dogs grieve too. Although he'd been there at the graveside when we buried Gus, Harley didn't seem to understand. For a few weeks he'd trot out to the car and check the back seat every time we arrived home. Eventually he seemed to accept that Gus wasn't coming back. But he was never the same. That winter he started to slow down—on the bush track around the cemetery he would walk well out of his way to skirt logs that he'd previously jumped over. I suspected that he was in pain. I took him to the vet and she agreed that he seemed to have injured his back.

As a pup, Harley had suffered mild epileptic seizures for a while. They were really just tics—his back legs would kick out involuntarily—but it was clearly uncomfortable and confusing for him. Usually quite an independent dog, he would seek me out as each attack was starting, and we would sit on the sofa, Harley across my lap (he was already a good twenty kilos by then), and I'd comfort him until the attack subsided and he drifted off to sleep. It was the start of a lifetime habit. Any illness or hurt—conjunctivitis, a prickle in a paw-pad—he would come to me and present the offending bit so I could fix it.

So now he would come to me and lean his lower back against me, but there was nothing I could do.

The vet prescribed an anti-inflammatory, which appeared to help a little for a while. But in October, as we were preparing for our trip to the Tasmanian Art Craft Fair where Hansa exhibited his vases every year, Harley deteriorated further. He was panting more than usual, and became very inactive. We'd already arranged to leave him with friends in Gembrook, Victoria, on the way down to Melbourne where we would catch the ferry to Tasmania. I was torn between wanting to do what was best for this beloved dog, and wanting to help Hansa at the busy fair. In the end I decided that I was worrying too much, and went ahead with the original plan; we left Harley with Jill and Pete. From the moment we left Gembrook I felt a mass like a lead ball in my stomach. Hansa's stall at the fair was busier than ever but I worried about Harley constantly. Every day I rang Jill to check. She tried to allay my fears but I knew that he was dying.

After six days we drove back up Jill and Pete's drive with trepidation.

Harley came to greet us, his head hanging low, his tail hardly wagging. Jill told me they'd tried everything but he hadn't eaten for two days. I thought, *fair enough, too, old friend. You felt like shit and I took you away from home and left you alone in an unfamiliar place with unfamiliar people. You decided to check out.*

I'd also forgotten how cold it could be in Gembrook in November—I hadn't packed his jacket and he was shivering as we said our goodbyes. Hansa helped him into the van, we turned the heater on high, and we brought him home. The next morning I called the vet again. That afternoon she put him to sleep.

My grief at losing Harley was only deepened by remorse at how he'd spent his last week. Jill and Pete had tried to keep him comfortable, but he should have been at home. Try as I might to remind myself of the happy, even idyllic, eleven years he'd had in Quaama with me and Gus, I wept again and again at thoughts of his last few days. I weep again now as I write this—it's been the hardest part of this story to recount.

Why would Harley's death play so heavily on me? I mean, why was this event so hard to recount? Harder than, say, the death of my mother?

I have always felt a deep love for my pets, but more—a profound responsibility for their safety and welfare. As a small girl I had dolls and I took their care very seriously too. I would create comfortable little homes for them in boxes. I would have wrapped them in cotton wool, if I'd had enough. It was important that they *were* safe, but also that they *felt* safe. I had seen my friend Simone's dolls, in her bedroom in Violet Street, cast in a corner, naked and forgotten, and I was aghast.

I have wondered, over the years, what Harley was thinking those long, cold six days in Gembrook—that I had abandoned him? Well, I suppose I had.

So my guilt hung over me. That, the days of anxiety I spent in Tasmania, and the weeks of concern beforehand, had again shifted my MS into overdrive—by February 2011 I needed my walking stick almost all the time.

***

In January 2012, my friend Akshara emailed me—'Sahi, have you seen this?'—with a link to a YouTube video by an American doctor called Terry Wahls. Wahls had MS, secondary progressive MS like me, but she claimed to have reversed her symptoms in nine months by changing her diet.

It certainly wasn't the first time I'd read about a new MS cure on the internet. The net is rife with instant cures for MS, and usually I would just roll my eyes and click the 'Back' button. But Wahls was a doctor, like George Jelinek. The science behind her diet appeared to be valid. And perhaps most of all, she'd started noticing improvements after just three months.

Before the diet, Wahls spent most of her days in a wheelchair and could walk short distances with two canes. After three months on the diet her condition started to improve. After nine months, she rode her bicycle eighteen miles.

The other dietary intervention I'd implemented for my MS—the Jelinek diet—was a leap of faith. What

I mean is that although I had a strong belief in its scientific basis, I could never be sure if it was doing anything. My disease was still progressing, but it may have progressed a lot faster without it. I would never know.

But here was a treatment plan that might well produce results—improvement, no less—in just a few months. Even if the results took longer to manifest, say six months, it was worth a try.

Wahls's diet was prescriptive to say the least. Three cups of this every day, one cup of that … mostly coloured vegetables. I decided to implement it in stages: I would start, in the autumn of 2012, with three cups a day of dark, leafy greens—really just a large salad. It was a decision that would prove to be most fortuitous.

I'd been suffering bouts of neuralgia since 2009. These manifested as pulses of intense pain, the kind of pain that would have had me begging for morphine—if it were constant. But it wasn't. Each pulse lasted a split second, then quickly faded away. Then it would happen again a few seconds later, or a minute later, or ten minutes later. And again, and again. A typical attack started slowly, built up to a three-second cycle, then slowed down again—usually over a few hours but sometimes longer. There's no sleeping when this is happening. Life would slow right down with all my focus on the point of the pain, often counting the seconds between the pulses, always anticipating the next one.

The site of this pain varied but it was usually on my left side. Sometimes it was in my ribcage, sometimes the side of my neck, or behind my ear.

Neuralgia doesn't respond to common analgesics—aspirin, paracetamol, ibuprofen. Opiates work, but I'd tried those once; it took me a year to wean myself off them, with some very unpleasant withdrawal symptoms. I'd sworn never to resort to them again.

By May 2012, when I started the new diet, I was having at least one debilitating attack of neuralgia a week. But within two weeks of starting those three cups a day of greens, I realised something: no neuralgia. Just an anomaly, I decided. But a month later, I was still free of it.

By the end of October I'd implemented most of the components of the Wahls diet. I'd bought a Vitamix blender, a commanding presence on the end of the kitchen bench. I was having a breakfast smoothie every day, ticking off quantities of leafy greens and coloured fruits and vegetables. Hansa was enjoying these too.

I have to say that I found the diet quite laborious. I estimated that I was spending, on average, ninety minutes more per day preparing meals—over and above the usual. But I was enjoying my food much more. I was looking forward to the huge salads at lunchtime, whereas before the diet I sometimes skipped lunch completely due to lack of interest. Now I would look at what I'd prepared and sense how good it was for me. Part of this may have been that we'd decided to start buying organic vegetables—if I was going to be eating these quantities of fruits and vegetables, I didn't want to be contaminating myself with the corresponding quantities of pesticides and other sprays used in chemical farming.

***

In early 2012, I ordered a mobility scooter from a wholesale company in Brisbane. The following week it arrived in a crate, which we broke apart to reveal a sleek, silver machine with a seat like a lounge chair and a thirty five kilometre range per battery charge. Unlike regular mobility scooters with their unforgiving, solid tyres, it had inflatable tyres and proper spring suspension. It was billed as 'semi all terrain'—whatever that means. But, as I quickly found, it took dirt roads and paddocks in its stride.

My main impetus in buying the scooter had been to walk Rudy. Rudy's a Rhodesian ridgeback, like Harley and Gus; we drove up to the Central Coast to claim him from a breeder a few months after Harley died. I'd still felt Harley's absence like a hole in the house, and I thought it could be filled. It couldn't—I still miss

Harley, and Gus, years later—but in 2012 I had this huge, clumsy, sweet but lazy hound with a tendency to gain weight. He needed his daily walk. Later that year we took in Benji, a rescue terrier, a duplicitous yet charming rogue, stealthy yet engaging—the character you'd expect of a dog that had survived solo on the streets of seaside Kiama for a few weeks, and my first experience with a small(ish) dog.

At first I thought that Benji might take advantage of the scooter's foot-plate for rests when his much shorter legs tired on our trips around the village. But he's a spirited little thing and we soon started to raise laughs along the way, Benji out ahead like a sleigh dog, and Rudy, 'Officer Plod' I call him, bringing up the rear.

Sadly, I must keep both dogs on the lead, Rudy after a couple of tragic chook-related incidents—he's a hunting dog, after all—and Benji because we missed those first few months of his development, that vital window when you can instil the 'recall' in a pup. And he has resisted all attempts at training since. If let loose he races in erratic circles, the winds of freedom in his shaggy coat (and the memory of discarded fish and chips in his nose), and if you chase him he looks back over his shoulder and grins—'Oh, good, you're coming too!'—and runs even harder.

It's always interesting to see the responses of able-bodied people to the scooter. Gushing admiration—

'Aren't these fabulous!', caressing the handlebars. *Mmm, they're great,* I think. Or, 'I'd kill for one of these some days!' *Sure, swap you for your legs?* Of course my snide, ungrateful thoughts remain unexpressed. I just smile and agree. But if someone's beaming down at you from on top of two serviceable legs, and telling you how lucky you are to have a mobility scooter, the gratitude can wear a little thin.

And sometimes there's an assumption that I must be lacking in common sense, to boot. My osteopath has a property two kilometres west of Quaama, a pleasant jaunt on the scooter in good weather. The trip takes me across the Princes Highway. The speed limit on the highway there is 100 kph—the traffic whooshes past. But the scooter can do 15 kph on the flat and there's good visibility in both directions.

So I was about to cross the highway one day, returning from the osteopath's, all loose and limber. In my mirror I noticed a four-wheel drive waiting behind me, then I took off. The four-wheel drive overtook me on the other side of the road, continued up the hill then stopped at the Quaama store. The driver got out and watched me pull up.

'Whoa!' he said. 'We were really worried! From where we were, we couldn't see if there was anything coming, then off you went!'

I told him he needn't have worried; I wouldn't have crossed if there were anything coming.

'Well, at least if you'd had any trouble, I had two nurses in the car!'

Really, I assured him, I wouldn't have crossed if there'd been anything—*anything at all*—on the highway.

'OK,' he said, shrugging. 'Well, you made it, and that's the important thing.'

Grrr.

* * *

During the first few months of 2013 I was plagued by urinary tract infections (UTIs). Or maybe it was just the one infection that never quite went away. And, as if UTIs aren't already unpleasant enough with the burning and frequency of urination, they're a double whammy for someone with MS: the urgency. When you don't move too fast that can be disastrous. There were times I never strayed too far from the toilet. And having only one kidney only added to my concerns, of course.

Participating in an MS Society teleconference on bladder and bowel problems, I described my symptoms, which by then included getting up in the night almost hourly, trouble urinating at times, and, paradoxically, urge incontinence too. Before it happened to me I'd always imagined incontinence (if I imagined it at all) as a slow leakage problem. Maybe for some it is. But I was fine and dry until I got the 'need to go' signal, then I didn't have a lot of time to act. There was no 'Hmm, I might think about finding a bathroom soon'. It was more like, *Get me to the porcelain and no-one's gonna get hurt.* This affliction had plagued me for a decade or more, since the days of Levi's 501s—but MS quickly cured me of button flies.

The teleconference presenter encouraged me to visit Professor Richard Millard, a urologist with a specialty in 'MS bladder' who ran a monthly clinic at the MS Society in Lidcombe, NSW.

I knew what was coming. Back in 1999 I'd consulted a continence nurse at the MS Society because from time to time I sat down to pee and, well, nothing happened. I knew my bladder was full, but ... nothing. That day the nurse listened briefly to my woes then announced that I would need to learn Clean Intermittent Self-Catheterisation, as she opened a drawer and flourished a plastic-wrapped length of surgical-type tubing. It looked like something a whitegoods repairman might carry in his stock of spare parts.

Keep in mind that I was, at that stage, otherwise almost symptom-free. I often had sore knees—MS-damaged nerves can make muscles spasm, and my calf muscles were constantly in a mild spasm, tightening my tendons too. And there was the fatigue, but that was it. Emotionally, I was still coming to terms with the diagnosis. And I was frazzled that day, running late after having to negotiate all the pre-Olympic Games roadworks of Homebush Bay in Sydney. I took one look at the catheter, excused myself and fled to the toilet, where I wept copiously (no problem with excreting fluids at that end) then sneaked out of the building without even saying good-bye.

Over the next fourteen years I endured worsening incontinence, avoiding basic life activities like seeing movies and driving long distances, mumbling excuses when removing myself from meetings and extended conversations ... sometimes short conversations. Often it was easier to just stay at home. On the occasions I did venture out, Hansa or another friend would perform reconnaissance at new places and sidle up to me, whispering, 'First corridor, third door on the left' or 'Behind the red-brick building', so I never needed to hunt when I needed the toilet.

In 2004 I had consulted a urologist in Melbourne, a young female specialist who'd impressed me on Radio National's *Health Report* talking about research on the clitoris. She was brusque and businesslike and wore Doc Martens. She referred me for a 'urodynamic study'. It was mortifying. I lay stirruped on a steel table, my bladder filling through a catheter from a fluid bag on a pole. 'Lie back and think of England,' I told myself, trying and failing to see the funny side. I was told to hold on until I absolutely couldn't. And then they tilted the table and I could let go—of the contents of my bladder and a flood of tears, of relief and humiliation.

After studying the scans the doctor told me I had a 'residual volume'—the amount left after I'd 'voided'—of about 150 ml. Disrupted nerve impulses to my bladder were leaving the muscle walls weak and it wasn't emptying as it should. This was the reason for my frequent visits to the toilet: my bladder only emptied partially, so, as it refilled, it was constantly pulling the 'need to go' trigger. The urologist prescribed a medication which helped a little with the urgency, if not the 'residual'.

The constant volume of urine left over was also causing the bladder infections. And those infections required extended courses of antibiotics. I knew, even then, that this was no good for my gut. Something had to give.

At our local Four Winds Classic Music Festival in 2012 I bumped into a friend from the local MS support group. She'd noticed that it wasn't the first time that day I'd had to visit the toilet (it might have been the fifth) and started to extol the virtues of self-catheterisation, the procedure I'd shirked all those years. Normally I'd appreciate advice from a fellow MSer but we happened to be surrounded by a few of her friends, one of whom was a teacher I worked with as a volunteer in a literacy program at Quaama School.

'Thanks, Trish,' I said. 'That's really interesting but maybe another time?' The other women were studying their programs, or their feet.

But Trish was on a mission. 'I had no idea how full my bladder was! You really must give it a go, Jen.'

Luckily the next act started tuning up on the stage. I excused myself and hurried back to my seat.

***

So here I was in July 2013, back at the MS Society in Lidcombe. Professor Millard, the urologist, was a small, very elderly man who sat cradled in a high-backed chair. During our extended consultation I watched him slide further and further down until the collar of his tweed jacket perched like a hood over his head. He looked, I mused, like a small, wizened Obi Wan Kenobi. But I was just trying to distract myself. The renal ultrasound I'd arranged the week before had confirmed that my bladder still had a large residual volume. There was a new-generation drug I could try but no more evasion; I would need to learn to self-catheterise.

A month later I visited a continence nurse at Moruya Hospital, an hour up the highway from Quaama. No, I'm not going to go into the intimate details of self-catheterisation here. You can Google it. There are videos on YouTube. But after some initial setbacks, I was soon catheterising for Australia, and it turned my life around. Okay, maybe I'm exaggerating a bit. But it's quick and painless, and disposable catheters mean that I can do it anywhere there's a cubicle with a basin for handwashing beforehand (that's the 'Clean' part of Clean Intermittent Self-Catheterisation). So, suddenly I could go to the cinema and watch a full-length movie without hobbling out halfway through and missing ten minutes of the story. I could go to concerts; I went to see Leonard Cohen in Wollongong later that year (he was glorious). It really did open up my life again.

And, after having four or five urinary tract infections a year, since starting self-catheterisation three years ago I've had only one infection. And yes, it was a doozy and led to a hospital admission I detail later, but still—just the one.

I found it hard, at first, to identify the perverse but deep feeling of satisfaction that came over me—still comes over me—when I catheterised. Then it came to me: in a life that sometimes feels at the mercy of a relentlessly malign process, here is one area that I've clawed back some control.

8. this strange but welcome change

During the next two years, I travelled many roads—scenic routes, U-turns ... dead ends. Much of this chapter is medical in nature and covers various treatments I pursued, both Western and complementary. It may be of interest to those in the MS community.

By the winter of 2013 my balance had deteriorated further, as had my lower-limb co-ordination. So I was less confident when walking, and it was taking longer to get anywhere. But perhaps more worryingly, I'd developed a mild tremor in my hands. I noticed it most when eating or drinking. My Melbourne neurologist picked it up during that classic test where you have to touch your nose then the doctor's finger, back and forth, rapidly. I'd always felt like a child doing that. Now I felt like a clumsy child.

I was also losing my signature. My lovely fishhook 'J' was coming out looking cramped and bent. My handwriting in general was becoming a hand scrawl. I'd started typing even personal notes to friends. Even then, I was mis-keying more often.

All this seemed to be coming on quite fast. Too fast. Playing on my mind was the realisation that upper-limb control, more even than lower-limb, was key to my independence. If I lost the use of my legs and was confined to a wheelchair I could still feed myself and even prepare meals. I might need help getting into the shower but once there I'd be able to take care of myself. Same for the toilet. In a wheelchair I could still read, write, use a computer. In fact, I sometimes caught myself staring wistfully at wheelchairs—the end of effort, the end of leg pain (I'm sure that if I do end up in a wheelchair I'll have words for that former self). But if I lost the use of my hands, my independence would go too.

I became depressed and my GP put me on a mild anti-anxiety medication. I visited my solicitor and made sure I had in place an Advanced Care Directive, a document that detailed my wishes in case I was hospitalised and couldn't communicate them myself, to save Hansa from having to make decisions on my behalf. It also stated that in the case of cancer or kidney failure I didn't want any treatment other than medications that would make me as comfortable as possible until I died. No surgery, no chemotherapy, no dialysis. I signed this document with a sense of relief. I gave copies to Hansa and the medical centre, reassured that serious illness could spell my escape from a future that felt hopeless—a morphine-infused exit plan.

I wasn't suicidal, but I was watching the euthanasia debate with mounting interest. It's a measure of my despondency at the time that any prospect of its legalisation lifted my spirits. Out in public, I used to play a mental game: was there anyone I could see that I wouldn't happily trade lives with? That morose teenage girl at the bus-stop? Sure. That obese young boy in the doctor's waiting room? No worries. That middle-aged lady in the café trying to calm her rowdy grand-kids? In a heartbeat.

I didn't want to be dead—I just didn't want to be me.

So by now I was willing, for the first time, to consider dicey therapies. Now, the risk of death seemed less daunting than the risk of becoming dependent on others for my daily needs. It was in this frame of mind that I headed to the Canberra consulting room of a specialist whose name I'd heard associated with stem cell therapy in Australia—a fairly risky procedure involving a full 'reset' of the immune system. I got straight to the point. Was I a candidate?

I'd heard this neurologist described as 'maverick'. Late middle-aged, he had a shock of blondish-grey hair and a wide mouth with generous lips which curled up a little at the corners, giving the unfortunate appearance of a permanent smirk. But he turned out to be a conscientious and compassionate doctor, excited by the developments in MS research and keen to find a solution for someone in that easy-to-dismiss MS stage: secondary progressive.

This doctor had been spurned by other neurologists for his willingness to investigate fringe treatments for MS. That's what attracted me. Too often, I found, doctors feared the disapproval of their peers and stayed on a narrow path of treatments favoured by pharmaceutical company trials.

But what he had to say about stem cell therapy, at least in Australia, was not promising. He'd been conducting stem cell treatments on MS patients for a few years at his hospital, with good results, when the hospital's ethics department closed down the program.

An episode of the SBS show *Insight* that aired soon after my first visit to this doctor raised the exciting prospect of a stem cell trial at St Vincent's in Sydney, but candidates were strictly limited to young patients who'd had MS only a few years, were on a fast track to disability and weren't responding to existing therapies. Stem cell therapy was established in Russia; they were accepting a wider range of patients (and charging a lot) but only those patients with short duration of disease were getting good results. I started letting go of even the Russian option.

First the neurologist suggested that I try a chemotherapy agent that had been shown to be effective in patients with active inflammatory lesions. But did I have active inflammation? An MRI the following week said no.

Plan B: he suggested I try Gilenya—fingolimod—a new oral medication. Gilenya works by reducing immune cell levels, thus reducing inflammation. I went home and consulted Google again, finding much information on Gilenya's application to relapsing-remitting MS, but none on its use in secondary progressive MS.

Initially confused, I decided to trust his judgment—mostly because I believed Gilenya to be my last option. I had to be assessed by an ophthalmologist (fingolimod has been known to cause macular oedema—a collection of fluid in the back of the eye causing blurry vision that resolves upon stopping the drug but can take some months) and have blood tests done before I started; I passed these assessments and returned to the neurologist.

He wrote my script and I took the opportunity to ask a question that had been troubling me. 'Why can't I find any evidence for the efficacy of Gilenya in secondary progressive MS?'

He looked at me happily—or was it just the smirk?—and said, 'Because there *is* none.'

I started on the Gilenya. I spent six hours after taking my first dose in a room at the local medical centre so the nurse could monitor my heart rate—there is evidence that Gilenya can slow a patient's heart rate dangerously during the first few hours of administration.

Gladly, there was no adverse effect—on my heart rate. But in the following weeks I started having breakthrough attacks of neuralgia, despite rigorous adherence to my leafy greens. My hand tremor had increased to the degree that one day at a lunch party I slopped a glass of (non-alcoholic) punch into a friend's lap. I was experiencing 'brain-fog' every day, making it very hard to work. I experienced trouble swallowing and choked three times, which was frightening. And I knew there was scant evidence, if any, that the drug would do anything for me. Maybe I'd embarked on my course of Gilenya with some pessimism, but after six weeks I weaned myself off it, ceasing it completely within eight weeks. One by one, anything this doctor offered me had come to nought.

It did occur to me that the time to employ pharmaceuticals had been when I was first diagnosed. Hindsight, they say, is always 20/20. I'd rejected my neurologist's advice to take Avonex back in 1998. If I knew then what I know now I would have overcome my needle phobia and started on Copaxone instead. Copaxone (glatiramer acetate) is a synthetic drug that modulates immune cells. Being synthetic, it doesn't invoke the flu-like reactions of the interferon therapies like Avonex. There might have been injection-site reactions. But a recent fifteen-year study found that patients on Copaxone had only progressed, on average, 0.6 points on the Expanded Disability Status Scale, a method of measuring disability in MS. In the last fifteen years I have progressed six points.

The company that supplies Copaxone is not one of those pharmaceutical giants with huge marketing budgets, so it was not usually the first drug suggested by a specialist, historically. But word of its success appears to be getting out. When talk at MS gatherings turns to medications these days, it seems to be the drug most prescribed.

If I were one to have regrets, I suppose I would regret not going on Copaxone. But I really don't give it a lot of thought. When I do, I remember my mild symptoms and the optimism I felt when I read George Jelinek's book, balanced against the injections and their side effects, and I understand my reticence, and my confidence.

* * *

It was around this time I heard about Rituxan. Jenn, a friend from the gym, had visited a specialist MS neurologist in New York. She'd paid US$2000 for three hours of his expert attention—you can do that in New York. After a comprehensive interview and physical examination, he'd recommended Rituxan, a monoclonal antibody. The New York specialist had been treating secondary progressive MS patients with Rituxan and had been getting good results. Many patients had stopped progressing; some had regained some ability.

Go back to Australia, he told Jenn, and get your neuro to prescribe Rituxan. He wrote her a letter to take to her physician.

So Jenn returned to Australia, excited and optimistic, and made an appointment to see her neurologist. His response was deflating, to say the least. In Australia, Rituxan was approved for use but only for certain conditions, such as rheumatoid arthritis. It was 'off-label' for MS. Off-label prescribing means prescribing a registered medicine for a use that is not included or is disclaimed in the product information. It's not illegal in Australia but doctors can be deterred by a number of clinical, safety and ethical issues.

I believe that Australia's health system, with its universal coverage and good value for money, is far superior to the US system. But we pay for its affordability with somewhat less flexibility. A doctor can't just write a script for any registered drug for any condition; there's a list of drugs that have been approved by our Therapeutic Goods Administration (TGA) for each condition. If a doctor, or a patient, wishes to try an 'off-label' drug, they need permission from the TGA.

Then, of course, the patient must pay for it. Jenn told me that Rituxan, if we could source it, would cost about $5000 for one 1000mg infusion. It seems that we could need four. I could afford that. So at my next visit, in January 2015, I asked the neurologist about Rituxan.

He started shuffling through a pile of papers on a corner of his desk, put on his glasses and started reading. 'Hmm, 22 SPMS patients ... 38 per cent demonstrating stability, 45 per cent improved' ... here he glanced at me and turned a page, '... 62.5 per cent reduction in progression ... overall safe and well-tolerated ... Of course, it's off-label in Australia for MS'

He passed me the papers and ... smirked? No, he was *smiling*. 'Now, how can we get around this off-label business?'

I felt buoyed by his interest. 'Can you prescribe it for me? Can you get approval from the TGA?'

He chuckled. 'Oh, no, no, no,' he said. 'It's only approved for rheumatoid arthritis. We'll have to find a friendly endocrinologist to prescribe you some. Leave it with me.'

I went home and waited. But a few months later all avenues, again, had led to dead ends. Perhaps my maverick neurologist was losing his nerve.

* * *

By July 2014 I'd been on the Wahls diet for well over a year and it was time to take stock.

My neuralgia was still just a memory—a bad one—except for four 'breakthrough' attacks, each of which I could attribute to easing up on the three cups daily of leafy greens. Sometimes it was because I was travelling, sometimes just bad planning, but if I missed more than two days of greens the pain would come back. So the end of the neuralgia was a life-changing result and would have been enough in itself for me to maintain the complete Wahls diet forever—except that I knew it was specifically the leafy greens that had done the job, not the other six daily cups of fruits and vegetables (I did have one severe neuralgia attack in 2015, but I attributed that to an undiagnosed, longstanding urinary tract infection. As I said, I'll regale you with that episode later. After four days in hospital on intravenous antibiotics, the infection cleared and the neuralgia petered out).

My Melbourne neurologist had previously prescribed an anticonvulsant—an epilepsy drug—for the neuralgia but it had made me drowsy and muddle-headed. In 2012 I had told him about the leafy greens.

'Ah, it must be the folate,' he said, instantly reducing a plate of luscious, crispy, organic nutrients to an isolated chemical component. But I'd tried folate—Vitamin B9. It wasn't folate, or not *just* folate. I tried to suggest to him that scientists haven't yet identified every single chemical in leafy green plants, and who knows what effect may be had by enjoying the combined effects of the whole food? But he was glazing over.

The neuralgia was the only real improvement I could pin down to the Wahls diet—as far as MS symptoms were concerned. But my overall health was good. Of course, I felt good in the knowledge that I was eating well and this was important. But there were other things. My skin, nails and hair were in great condition. People kept saying, 'You look so well!' (Of course, when you have MS, people are always telling you how well you look. It's what they say when they're thinking, 'She walked all the way to the bathroom!' or 'She's standing up!')

Since realising that the Wahls diet wasn't going to cure my MS, I have eased up on its demands, mostly due to the time required every day to comply with it. But the plate of leafy greens is a daily fixture, and I'll always be grateful to Dr Wahls for that discovery.

Calorrr, dolorrr, rrruborrr, tumorrr: Latin for heat, pain, redness, swelling—the four signs of inflammation—in the thick, *rrr*olling Scots accent of my second-year pathology professor. All that was fairly academic when applied to MS, where the inflammation is internal and invisible without scans. But I did know that reducing inflammation to any degree had to be a good thing for my MS—and my overall health. Sugar feeds harmful microbes in the gut, like *Candida albicans*, which outcompete the beneficial ones, creating an imbalance and leading to inflammation. For this reason I gave up sugar in October 2014, embarking on the anti-candida diet for three bland months.

Within a month, two things happened. *Catalyst*, ABC TV's science program, broadcast a show on gut flora. It was the first time I'd heard of a link between the beneficial microbes colonising the human gut, and the immune system. While I was still digesting (sorry) this new information, I had a session with my counsellor.

Entering Lisa's office, I noticed the change in her at once. She was thin and gaunt and pale. 'What happened?' I asked her, shocked.

She sighed. 'Long story.'

She'd been admitted to hospital a few weeks previously suffering severe stomach cramps and fever. Her condition was so severe that she was quickly transferred to the High Dependency Unit, where she spent five days drifting in and out of consciousness with a diagnosis of peritonitis. When she'd regained consciousness enough to talk to a doctor she was horrified to learn that they'd performed exploratory surgery and removed her appendix. She questioned the need for this, as she hadn't had appendicitis. She was told that yes, her appendix was 'very healthy', but they thought they 'might as well remove it while they were in there'. They thought they were doing her a favour.

Recovering slowly in the next few weeks, Lisa did some research about the human appendix and discovered that it was far from the redundant, vestigial organ she was taught about at school, a remnant from our predecessors whose diet was rich in foliage. In fact, it was now considered a vital part of our digestive system. Among other functions, it's a store of beneficial microbes that the gut can use to re-inoculate itself after a crisis such as heavy antibiotic use or a gastric illness. And now she'd lost hers, just when she most needed it—she'd been administered high dose intravenous antibiotics for five days.

She immediately started researching how, in the absence of an appendix, she could repopulate her gut with beneficial bacteria. Her search landed her on the doorstep of ex-CSIRO scientist Robert Gourlay in Mongarlowe, NSW.

Gourlay's specialty at CSIRO had been environmental health, specifically the microbial health of soil and waterways. But since retirement he'd diversified into human health—specifically gut flora—and now supplied a range of liquid probiotics.

Lisa had seen the *Catalyst* program too. 'Jen,' she said, leaning forward, 'you *must* talk to Robert Gourlay.'

I did, and by May 2015 had been dosing myself morning and night for five months.

Like many, I'd taken probiotics in capsule form for years, mostly the *Lactobacillus acidophilus* and *L. bifidobacterium* strains. I'd never noticed any difference but believed they must be doing some good. On Gourlay's probiotic, however, I was noticing clear benefits. I'd been constipated for years—a symptom of 'MS lazy gut', where the muscles of the intestine spasm and digestion takes far too long. Or so I thought. But now I could face that part of my life with far less trepidation—ah, the sheer aesthetic pleasure of an easy evacuation! And often on *consecutive days*, no less.

But if this new joy in the bathroom wasn't enough, there was a change in me even more profound—I was starting to feel happy again. I'd noticed a marked improvement in my state of mind—and May was when, in the past, my mood would usually start slumping with the shorter, darker, cooler days, less time outdoors and knowing that winter was on the way. I really don't like being cold. It wasn't usually the time of year that I would wake up feeling a sense of optimism, but now I was rising from bed looking forward to the day ahead.

It was only after I'd noted this strange but welcome change in mood that I started spotting media stories about the link between gut health and mental health. Later that month I was reading *The Monthly* and was surprised to turn the page to see an article about the human microbiome, *Gut Feelings,* by Jo Chandler. Surprised, because although I'd long subscribed to this magazine to enjoy great journalism on Australian politics, society and the arts—its claimed remit—I didn't expect to see a story on gut health. Wow, I thought, the microbiome really has made it, if *The Monthly* devotes eight pages to it.

I devoured the story. After all, I was becoming quite the evangelist on gut health amongst my friends, boring and disgusting them in equal measure, and here was more material. But just two pages in, I read something that made me sit up: '… the interplay of bugs in the gastro-intestinal tract with the central nervous system, and how it might influence neurobiology and conditions like Alzheimer's, Parkinson's, autism, schizophrenia and anxiety'. I'd read about gut flora for digestion and gut flora for the immune system. But gut flora for neurological health? For mental health?

Suddenly it seemed I couldn't read a newspaper or turn on the radio without hearing about gut health, or probiotics, or the microbiome. On 11 July Gail Bell reviewed German scientist Giulia Enders' *Gut: The Inside Story of Our Body's Most Under-rated Organ* in the Sydney Morning Herald's *Spectrum* lift-out. I downloaded *Gut* onto my Kindle that night.

On 13 July on Radio National's *Health Report*, Dr Norman Swan interviewed Dr Peter Turnbaugh of the Department of Microbiology and Immunology, University of California, about gut flora's effect on obesity. On 18 August on RN's *All in the Mind* (you can tell I'm an RN girl, can't you?) Lynne Malcolm and Olivia Willis discussed 'Why the gut has been dubbed our "second brain"'. I sat glued to this program—it confirmed for me that my improved mood and outlook in the past few months, rather than just a coincidence, may well have been a result of Gourlay's brew. After all, as I learned that day, ninety percent of the body's neurotransmitters, such as the feel-good hormone serotonin, are produced in the gut—not by our own cells, but by our microbiota. It was on this program that Dr David Perlmutter (*Brain Maker*, Little, Brown, 2015) made another connection, that 'the gut and the bacteria that live within the gut regulate the process of inflammation in the human body'. Damn, it looked like I'd have to give up sugar again—after my brilliant result earlier that year I'd gradually reintroduced sugar into my diet. The spirit was strong …

Next, my gym friend Liz sent me a link to a 2014 article in *Scientific American*: 'Could Multiple Sclerosis Begin in the Gut?' It mentioned various studies that had found differences in the gut flora of patients with MS compared with healthy subjects.

So, rebalancing my gut flora was possibly enhancing my mood and reducing the progression of my MS. If I wasn't sold before, I was now.

But there may have been another factor in all this. It's mysterious, it's esoteric, and I document it here because I have a gut feeling that it's relevant. And in the light of my probiotic experience, even the scientist in me is paying more heed to gut feelings.

9. where shame and MS collide

In April 2015 I participated in a one-day therapy workshop called Family Constellations, facilitated by my friend Tanmaya in Tilba Tilba, half an hour up the coast. On a cool Saturday morning, fifteen of us sat on chairs in a circle in Tanmaya's big living room while he explained briefly what would be happening that day.

Then he smiled and looked around the circle. 'Okay, who'd like to do a constellation?'

A woman moved to sit on the empty chair beside him, and he asked some questions: what issue would she like to look at today? ... Tell us a bit about your mother, your father ... then he invited the woman to choose other participants to represent those key players.

The representatives gathered in the centre of the circle and played out, under Tanmaya's loose direction, scenes and situations from the woman's life. The representatives knew only what the woman had said in her short conversation with Tanmaya. A lot of what eventuated in the circle appeared to be intuitive. The woman herself watched from her seat.

I kept glancing at her; she often nodded—whatever was happening seemed to strike a chord for her. She wept as Tanmaya directed the little play to its close.

On that April morning, Tanmaya completed constellations for two participants before we broke for morning tea. Friends had told me that the day could be emotionally intense, and they weren't wrong. Even as an observer I sensed the profound insights becoming apparent to the focal participant.

So, after morning tea, my heart in my mouth, I put my hand up and moved to sit in the chair next to Tanmaya.

He started by identifying the key influences in my early family life—obviously they were my parents—and I asked three participants to represent them and me. Then Tanmaya used his own intuition to bring in various other representatives from the circle, each in turn using their own instinct, and the quick sketch I'd provided, to play out scenarios guided by him. All I had to do was sit tight and watch.

The effect was mind-blowing. Whether it was Tanmaya's own intuitive powers, those of the various representatives or the intervention of the collective subconscious—hell, interplanetary influences, I don't care!—the drama playing out in the circle brought out insight after insight. But when Tanmaya chose someone to represent not a family member but my MS, the drama took an even more intense turn. By the time he invited me to stand up, enter the fray and face my 'father' I was clutching bundles of damp tissues. And the key finding was yet to come out.

My 'father' and I faced off, the other players grouped around us. Tanmaya turned to me. 'It was easier to get sick,' he said, 'than to stay angry'.

Even typing that now, it hits me like a gut-punch.

***

It was five months after starting on Gourlay's probiotic and a month after Family Constellations that I started noticing this new contentment, and optimism—and the regularity in the bathroom (for which I give no credit to Family Constellations).

I was happy with my current regime of supplements, able to identify the benefits of each and every tablet and capsule I was taking. Even my two prescription drugs—for muscle spasms and overactive bladder—were having notable effects. I was similarly happy with my exercise regime—Tuesdays with Jaimey at the gym as well as the half-hour daily workout he'd assigned me for home. Through my own lack of proaction my work levels had ramped down to a manageable, fairly stress-free level. I wasn't earning much, I admit, but enough to cover the supplements and consultations with Jaimey as well as the fortnightly three hours of a gardener's time that gave me peace of mind when wandering around my still rambling garden. And as I was receiving a part-pension, that's all I now asked of my work. Especially as I wanted more and more time to write.

I was writing more stories for our local community newspaper, *The Triangle* (named for the territory bounded by our three surrounding mountains). My involvement with *The Triangle* has never been limited to writing—it had started in 2003 when I'd fronted up to the paper's first AGM with a copy of the latest issue. I had marked up all the spelling, grammar and punctuation errors in red pen. The committee of the time looked at me blankly. What a pedant, they must have thought. But, 'Everyone,' announced the President, 'please welcome our new proof-reader, Jen Severn!' I soon progressed to layout artist and Quaama village correspondent.

The Triangle covers the usual small town stories—Country Women's Association successes, agricultural shows, school news, Rural Fire Service training days … art exhibitions and music events, book reviews and launches, recipes and gardening advice. It's not particularly racy or salubrious—our 'Pet of the Month' is a rescue dog needing a home—but it has been known to stray into contentious areas from time to time. Some friendly local lawyer or another usually gets us out of trouble on a pro bono basis when we need it.

There were a few sleepless nights many years ago when I decided to follow up a story involving an unpopular development proposal, poker machines and mysterious payments to Sydney management consultants. I came home one day to find rolls of shiny paper strewn across my office floor; a whistle-blower had anonymously faxed me three years of balance sheets and profit and loss statements from the organisation in question. I asked to interview the Chairman and arrived on the appointed day to find the entire Board present—florid-faced gents in suits, some of them sweating rivulets. The story made the front page that month but there was no come-back—the editorial committee had crossed all their t's, etc. And the development didn't go ahead. I'd love to think it was down to my girl-detective exposé but I suspect the venture was simply found to be unviable.

In 2014 I took on some similarly demanding (but less threatening) assignments such as covering talks at the Bermagui Institute Public Dinners. These dinners hosted identities of the calibre of independent ex-federal Member for New England Tony Windsor, ex-Treasury Secretary Ken Henry and Fairfax Economics Editor Ross Gittins, lured by our inestimable 'old Commie rabble-rouser' Jack Miller on the promise of a bottle of wine and a night's accommodation in Jack's spare room. I imagined these erudite speakers driving into town looking for an imposing, colonnaded building, and instead stumbling into the dining room of the Bermagui pub, where an enthusiastic, politically astute, decidedly left-leaning crowd of fifty or so awaited them. The 'Bermagui Institute' was a ruse. You'd think word would get out in those upper echelons of politics and economics, but no. In fact, I rather suspect these seasoned presenters enjoyed it, after their usual engagements speaking to stuffed shirts dining at lavishly-set tables in grand hotels—an audience often there more for the deal-making and networking than their own edification.

That year I received a 'Go for Gold Scholarship' from the MS Society. I wanted to work with a mentor, originally for a novel I was writing—about the inhabitants of a small rural village in dairy country, would you believe ... well, they do say, 'write what you know', and I certainly had some material. But episodes from my previous life kept breaking through, so I changed my focus and found a life-writing mentor. Now there was a whole Society expecting something from me. And my mentor, of course.

In December 2014 I started meeting another writer for supportive chats and to work on our respective short stories. This was becoming a strong, constructive partnership and was very useful for both of us. Sarah was a fellow member of the *Triangle* editorial committee and although I'd known her for years I hadn't known she was a writer—she'd limited her *Triangle* involvements to technical roles—until she showed me her entry for a local short story competition we'd both entered. By the time I'd read the first page I was entranced (that story was later published by *The Australian* in their 2016 *Summer Reading* supplement). I was delighted when Sarah suggested forming a writers' group. The 'group' ended up being just the two of us, but it suited us very well.

***

So that was my life in May 2015. I attributed my regained happiness and optimism to two factors—the probiotic and Family Constellations. Current findings leave no doubt as to the link between gut health and mental health. And I'm happy to assume that the Family Constellations workshop had a profound effect on my state of mind too, but I won't even start to try to explain it.

I realised at that time, too, that I'd stopped a habit I'd indulged in for many years—waking each morning wondering if today was the day that my MS would be cured. That it had quietly resolved in the night, having surrendered in the face of my constant sorties against it, and I would once again be nimble, strong and sturdy. My first few steps always led to disappointment, if a spasm hadn't already hit me as I rolled over. And disappointment was no way to start the day. But this didn't feel like resignation; it felt more like acceptance.

* * *

When I heard that Tanmaya was holding another Family Constellations workshop that November, I booked in straight away. Ever since the first workshop in April I'd been thinking about another issue I'd like to explore through this mysterious process.

Tanmaya may have sensed my enthusiasm as I sat in the circle that morning.

He was smiling. 'Sahi.' It wasn't a question.

I went to sit beside him. 'It's about shame,' I said.

* * *

Shame. 'I'm ashamed of you, Jennifer.' I'd grown up in the shadow of shame—my mother's, and by extension my own.

Mum grew up in poverty during and after the Second World War in London. She won a scholarship to a grammar school and, like me thirty years later, was very aware of her home and its deficiencies, in particular, compared with her school friends' houses. As an adult, she was very self-conscious and prone to feeling shame.

I understood shame from an early age. When I was four Mum enrolled me in the Cinderella Kindergarten, a short walk away from home, for two days a week. One day the teacher caught me talking during nap time and rapped me over the ankles with a long ruler. Years later, as an adult, I recounted the incident to Mum. It may have been in the context of a conversation about corporal punishment in schools.

Mum was shocked. 'Why on earth didn't you tell me?'

Well, I had to think about that. Maybe I thought she'd be angry with me for disobeying instructions. But more likely I thought she'd be ashamed of me, which was much harder to bear.

And here's where shame and MS collide for me: I can sometimes find myself paralysed by self-consciousness—literally. Self-consciousness and embarrassment are really just paler shades of shame. I can be walking along, slowly but steadily, then I'm brought up short by a thought, usually the idea that someone's watching. That someone's noticed my awkwardness, my lack of grace. My incompetence. And suddenly one foot feels glued to the floor. I falter, I stumble, I stall.

My counsellor gave me an awareness exercise to use in these situations. 'Take a deep breath, let it out slowly, and feel the ground under your feet,' she told me. 'Feel your weight, your connection to the floor, to the ground. Then start again.'

It works. But walking can still be a stop-start affair. I'd rather not feel the self-consciousness, the embarrassment—the shame—in the first place.

* * *

That morning at the Family Constellations workshop I told Tanmaya that I often felt ashamed—of things I'd said or done, the wrong thing, or at the wrong time.

'And now,' I said, 'I see my disability as a lack of competence. I'm awkward and graceless when I walk. The shame of it can paralyse me—stop me in my tracks.'

Tanmaya closed his eyes. 'When did this start? Do you remember shame as a child?'

'Yes, my mother was often ashamed of me. But she was ashamed of herself as well.'

'Her parents?' asked Tanmaya.

'Her mother was born in a workhouse in South London,' I said. This was my plump, affectionate Nana, who used to cook, sew and garden with me. 'It was a family secret. Mum's dad, my grandfather, didn't want anyone to know.'

I chose people from the circle to represent me, Mum, Nana and Poppa, and Tanmaya went to work.

I won't recount the dramas that played out in that room the next hour or so. But my lasting memory is of joining the group in the centre, at the end, and sinking back into the arms of my 'grandmother'—Nana, who in turn leaned into *her* mother, and so on down the chain for five generations. That's how far back Tanmaya had traced the shame. And as I settled into the warm cushion of my 'Nana' I let that chain of mothers take my entire weight—they were strong—and with it the shame. It seems it wasn't mine at all. Never was.

* * *

Writing this now, I'm trying to remember the last time I stalled while walking in public. I can't. And recently I ran my customary post mortem after a social event (some things may never change). I remembered some gaffe, and brushed it aside. No self-censure, no disappointment, no shame. Just a sense of wry humour and compassion, as one might feel for a loved, errant child.

* * *

One more thing, though, happened that day at Tanmaya's. After lunch, another woman did a constellation and invited me to represent her—herself—the star in her family drama. It was my first time representing and I resolved to fully engage in the part, to detach from my own issues and get in touch with whatever it was that other participants contacted when they played those significant but mysterious protagonists in other people's lives.

From the woman's conversation with Tanmaya I had gleaned that her father had often been absent from her family's life. And as the drama played out in the circle that day, her 'father' was, indeed, always just out of sight. I could see him from time to time, just within my peripheral vision, playing little or no part in the drama.

So when, towards the end, Tanmaya directed that father character to come closer and reconnect with the family group, I felt a surge of emotion. I'd been deeply immersed as the young girl with an absent father, and now here he was, the father, gazing at me, his face a study in remorse, and love, and promise for the future. He even *looked* like my father—*my* father. I dissolved into tears, my part in the drama forgotten.

Tanmaya must have known what was happening. Afterwards I checked with him. 'Did I hijack that woman's constellation?'

He reassured me. 'Sahi,' he said, 'it's uncanny but people are often chosen as reps because they resonate with the story, or because there are parallels with their own system. Maybe you were crying your own tears looking at your own father in that moment, but you were also crying the tears for her, that she hadn't yet been able to allow.'

I'll just have to trust that the poor woman still gained some insights to take away.

***

An event in September, a few weeks beforehand, had rocked my confidence a little. I'd been feeling quite well and buoyant, happy with my management plan … until the day the ambulance arrived.

Neuralgia. I've mentioned it before. A stab of intense pain, a sharp spike that radiates briefly and dissipates, then there's just the anticipation of the next one. Maybe a minute later, maybe thirty seconds, maybe three. At three seconds there's not much respite between the jabs. At times all that exists is the pain and the counting.

Previously I'd always had an attack in one location—under my ribs, or in the side of my neck, or the side of my head. But the neuralgia gods really went to town this time. As well as being more intense, the pain was in my ribs *and* my head. So there was no respite—as the jab in my ribs subsided, the one in my head went off.

After thirty-six hours of this, I was exhausted, weak and scared, and Hansa'd had enough of running hot baths and boiling heat packs, to no avail. It was time for the big guns.

The paramedics took my temperature—40.5. Clearly there was more to it than neuralgia. I told them I suspected a urinary tract infection, and infections can worsen MS symptoms. A urine test in Emergency confirmed it.

In the High Dependency Unit they started infusing broad-spectrum antibiotics and tried a range of analgesics. The waves of pain came and went at will. This neuralgia had assumed a personality of its own, and it was resilient.

Allow me, please, a moment of overwhelming gratitude for the HDU nurses at Bega Hospital. Rowena with the bleached hair, looking forward to completing her Critical Care Certificate in two weeks' time, met me and the neuralgia on admission to the unit, overseeing attempts with various drugs, but they didn't touch it. That attack subsided into a few hours of pain-free, endorphin-fuelled haze, as they do. Then the pain arose again to meet Sue, kind and motherly, back on staff from retirement to help out her daughter studying medicine in Canada. Later it greeted Leonie, candid and droll and good for spirited, cynical exchanges about the new Prime Minister in my lucid moments. It returned with a vengeance for Rob, gruff and competent but helpless in the face of my sudden tears, at the end of both his shift and my inner resources.

That's when, in a moment of despair, I sent out a plea.

It was a profound entreaty, a prayer. It was a measure of my desperation and went out to whatever gods, whatever guardian angels, whatever higher powers there were. Then I settled back and waited for the pain to stop. That's when Francesca came on late shift.

Francesca—a renaissance beauty with copper curls—a Botticelli angel. She massaged my feet, she re-positioned me in bed despite the tubes and wires, she placed a pillow between my knees, she rubbed my back. I fell deeply, deliciously asleep, and slept for eight hours, only elusively aware of her two-hourly ministrations—like surfacing briefly from a tropical lagoon before sinking again into its warm, shimmering depths.

By morning it was clear that something had shifted. They'd hit on the right drug, an opiate, something I'd avoided in the past but now I'd take anything. At first, five shots at five-minute intervals settled the pain, then three shots, then two. Then the waves slowed up, and the spikes were less severe. They transferred me to Medical Ward. Another attack started but Hansa had brought in a heat pack, which by now did the job.

I still held faith in my regime. But to my supplements, my diet, my intestinal health, my physical training and that handful of medications, I now added this:

the respect for my nearly fifty years of experience inhabiting this body, that when I go to a GP with a suspected urinary tract infection, armed with a urine specimen, and he does a dipstick test and a cursory abdominal examination and says it's muscular pain and to take some Panadol, I will insist gently that he send the specimen off to pathology. I was too polite, too deferring. That was two weeks before my admission and the infection had been brewing all that time.

10. a neat dovetail

There's a creature, an entity, that's taken up domicile in my innards. It's nestled next to my stomach, just under my diaphragm. In my mind's eye it's long and lithe and slippery, and muscled, like an eel.

Most of the time it lies dormant and I'm unaware of it. But then a thought wakes this beast—that mind-gut connection again. A visual of me, being spoon-fed; me, in bed, paralysed; me, contorted in a wrenching spasm; me, being helped onto the toilet.

It stirs and wraps itself, constrictor-like, around my stomach, which shrinks and hardens. It forces my diaphragm up, making my breath fast and ragged. It only ever stirs in the early hours; I'm in bed, Hansa's asleep beside me, and my imagination has free rein.

But I'm getting better at taming the beast. I remind my imagination that it's 2.35 am and these images are cowardly—they don't dare show their face in daylight hours. Then I think of what daylight will bring. Within hours I'll be making my own breakfast, or taking the dogs for a run, or working at my computer, or going to the gym, or meeting a friend for coffee. And the beast curls back up and settles into that crook against my stomach, under my diaphragm, and goes back to sleep.

* * *

When I first consulted that maverick neurologist in late 2013, the beast had been making its presence felt. My condition seemed to be progressing fast, fast enough that I was prepared to consider the risky stem cell treatment. But when I assess my condition now, almost three years later, maybe the progress isn't as fast as I was preparing for.

I've added aquatic exercise to my regime; last summer we visited the pool in Cobargo twice a week. I walked from one end to the other, twenty-five metres, forwards, backwards, sideways. In Cobargo Pool I can walk all the way to the deep end—on tiptoes. Remember, I'm tall. Over the summer I worked my way up to twenty laps, five hundred metres. It was such a joy to walk without my stick! I hadn't realised, until Hansa told me, that I'd been smiling the whole way. On days we didn't go to the pool I got on the stationary bike at home and pedalled four kilometres, or five on a good day, on the 'hill' rating of four (out of nine). Lately I'm doing those four kilometres faster. Jaimey has me on a high protein diet; he wants me to put on some muscle mass. His theory is that if I'm stronger it will improve my balance, and he's usually right so I'm going with it.

It's really my balance that's the biggest impediment to my walking. After ten years of using a stick, I've bought a walker. I've taken it out a handful of times—I appreciate it when I don't have Hansa's sturdy arm to lean on. That's when the one extra point of reference that the stick has afforded me sometimes doesn't feel like enough; I need to lean on something stable. And the inbuilt seat is a bonus—my very own dedicated pew, anywhere, anytime!

The tremor in my hands is a little worse than in 2013. If I raise my arms to eat with a fork or to drink from a glass, my hands will shake. Just a little. So I use both hands to hold a cup or glass, avoid soup, and trust my dining companions to forgive my clumsiness with knife and fork. My handwriting varies in legibility. My signature seems to differ every time—but these days there's not much to sign (prescriptions, mostly).

In summary, my condition has progressed, but minimally. When I think of my fears at that time, in late 2013, at how fast things seemed to be moving, at how soon I might become dependent on Hansa or professional carers for my everyday needs, I'm ahead.

* * *

When I was first diagnosed I had sore knees, strange sensations, bouts of fatigue. I thought, 'I can cope with this. I can't afford to get any worse, but I can deal with this.' Then I got a bit worse—some minor continence issues. I thought, 'It's okay, I can manage this. I can't afford to get worse … but I can cope with this.' Then I got a bit worse again, some balance issues … you guessed it. 'I can deal with this …' Nineteen years later and I'm still saying it, every time.

* * *

So, after all the various diets and therapies I've tried since I was diagnosed, I still have progressive MS. Some might say that all that dieting, denying myself foods that I would have loved to eat, the expense of the supplements and ten years of consultations with Jaimey have come to nothing. But I could be a lot worse—after all, I've had MS for nearly thirty years. And some health practitioners do seem surprised that I'm still on my feet at all.

That's the difficult thing with treating MS; its course is so unpredictable. Everything I've tried has been a leap of faith. I would love to try a new therapy or diet and know within days, or even months, if I'm feeling better. That was my attraction to Terry Wahls' regimen. But no, the best I've been able to do is assess the science and make an educated choice.

The probiotic, however, has proven beneficial for both my physical and mental health. If my MS slows down or stops progressing it could be for any number of reasons, including the sheer unpredictability of the disease. But my digestive system appreciates this daily brew, and as for my outlook, it has improved greatly.

I have a strong feeling, not that I'm *curing* my MS, but that I'm maintaining a holding pattern. I've slowed it down to the point that I'll be a contender for whatever new therapies may become available—as long as they become available soon.

And for someone with a chronic, degenerative condition I have a lot on my side. I have a comfortable house and a bit of cash in the bank thanks to my inheritance from Mum. I have my friends and a solid community around me. And I have Hansa.

For an artist, Hansa's pretty handy. He maintains both my electric scooters. He knocks up specialty gym equipment for me in his workshop. He welded castors onto a sturdy, upholstered bar stool so I can scoot effortlessly around the kitchen. He cleans, he cooks, he launders, he shops. He has taken over the vegetable garden, which was once my domain, so we can still have fresh produce (the sum total of my contribution to the gardening these days is the jar of alfalfa sprouts on the kitchen windowsill).

But Hansa's practicality is the smaller part of him. He's my moral and emotional support, a constant comfort when things seem too hard. One day early in our relationship I had to wait too long in a queue for a public toilet in Bega. I sat there feeling miserable, mortified and a little damp, while he went off to Target to buy me a fresh pair of knickers, coming back ten minutes later with dry underwear ... and a big bunch of flowers.

I don't mean to imply that Hansa's some kind of selfless angel, with no life of his own. His passion is fast cars (watching them, not driving them), and he often takes off for days—sometimes weeks—to enjoy the scream of turbocharged engines and the heady fumes of high-octane fuel. But he's usually around. He scouts ahead at new destinations, checking accessibility by foot or scooter. He walks up stairs behind me, and down stairs in front, in case I slip. That's Hansa—clearing the way, cushioning the falls.

***

The MS Society encouraged us all to register for the National Disability Insurance Scheme, and one bright day in early 2016 Barbara arrived in a flurry of federally-funded fervour, to work out my Goals and Personal Plan. I know I scoff, but as I sat on the sofa with her that day, piles of ring binders in our laps, the abundant options for support I may need in future years had a way of focusing my mind. What I wanted, above all else, was to continue to walk, to stay engaged in the community, and to write.

Nothing makes me feel as alive as writing does. Sometimes, when it's really flowing, I'm scribbling or tapping away and realise, with a great, heaving gasp, that I've stopped breathing—hard to say for how long.

When I can't walk, or even stand up, I sit down and write. When I'm in pain, I write. When I'm too exhausted to do anything else, I write. Writing takes me somewhere else when my body's an uncomfortable place to be. My physical world and my ability to participate in it may be shrinking but when I write I have no limitations.

* * *

I've said before that my attitude, since realising I'd like to continue to live, feels more like acceptance than resignation. But that doesn't mean I'll stop searching for ways to slow, or halt, or recover from, MS. If I'm going down, I'll go down swinging. Two inter-related avenues have crystallised for me recently: brain plasticity and meditation.

First to plasticity. Until recently, it was thought that brain cells were immutable. That once the brain was formed, the functions of its parts were hard-wired; if a part became damaged, the function of that part was irretrievably lost. But in the last fifty years or so, more and more evidence has shown the brain to be changeable—*plastic*—well into adulthood.

Since reading Canadian psychiatrist Norman Doidge's first book, *The Brain that Changes Itself*, I've been intrigued by the idea that conscious thoughts can make nerve cells forge new connections in the brain. For instance, just visualising the playing of a concerto, imagining her fingers moving across a keyboard, can improve a pianist's performance; visualising a complex sequence of cartwheels, arabesques and hand stands can polish a gymnast's floor routine. I started visualising walking—relaxed, fluid, co-ordinated walking. In my mind I would wander down the road and along bush tracks around the cemetery, often accompanied by Harley and Gus, my long-gone hounds. But I would do it in bed at night, and it was more a pleasant way to drift off to sleep than a therapeutic exercise.

When Doidge's next book came out—*The Brain's Way of Healing*, in 2015—I was excited to see that this time he'd recounted some stories of people affected by MS, and the improvements they'd experienced with a device called the Portable Neuromodulation Stimulator (PoNS).

The PoNS was developed in the laboratory of Dr Paul Bach-y-Rita, one of the first advocates of brain plasticity. It comprises a small, flat, lightweight panel of electrodes that sits on the tongue, held in place with the teeth. This is wired to a matchbox-sized control unit. Bach-y-Rita chose the tongue to receive his device's signals due to its sensitivity and proximity to the part of the brain called the pons (the acronym is no accident). The pons is part of the brain stem, a densely packed area at the top of the spinal cord; almost all signals between the body and the brain pass through it. It's closely connected with the areas of the brain that process movement and balance. The tongue, says Doidge, 'is a royal road to activating the whole human brain'. There are '15,000 to 50,000 nerve fibres on the tip of the tongue' alone.

In *The Brain's Way of Healing*, I read of MS patients recovering various abilities—balance, walking, running, singing, speaking, swallowing—after sessions using the PoNS. Some people experienced improved bladder function or better sleep or reduced tremor. Of course it's not a cure. The PoNS is helping the brain form new circuits to circumvent damaged ones. So someone with progressive MS would need to use the device for the rest of her life. But people were *regaining their abilities*. I'll definitely be watching out for a commercial model of the PoNS.

Now I come to meditation.

I go back again to the day of Mum's funeral at St Paul's, when the sight of Dad pulling into the carpark threw me off balance—literally, from one moment to the next. In the ten years since, the fact that my mind, to a large extent, can affect my balance and coordination has been a source of frustration to me.

There were those other moments: walking along in public and becoming aware of being watched, and faltering. At home I walk, slowly but confidently, without my stick, along the hallway (those walls are so reassuringly close!) or around the house, where a doorway or a piece of furniture is always there to grab if needed. But in an open space I'm left flailing, glued to the floor.

In each instance my mind has over-ridden my physical ability. I'd love to say it's *all* in the mind. It's not. But my challenge now is to find out exactly how much is.

Since my introduction to meditation in 1988, my practice had been patchy at best. In Pune in 1989 I took up 'Dynamic Meditation' and ended up in hospital with a kidney infection. In 1995 I did a ten-day, silent *vipassana* retreat (watching the breath) at a

Buddhist centre in Blackheath, NSW, and came out with a mental five-year plan for my wholesale jewellery business. There was that time in 1998-2000 doing *pranayama* breathing that led me naturally into a meditative state. I would sit for some time after each daily session. But it became less regular then fell away completely; I wasn't committed. Since then there've been sporadic attempts to create a regular practice, always giving way eventually to something more entertaining, even work.

One day in early 2016 the MS Society announced it was holding an online course on Mindfulness and Meditation. I wondered, after all those years of sitting with enlightened masters and gurus, if an MS Society webinar would have much to offer me, but I duly connected in at the appointed time to see a Victorian nurse explain the process and benefits of mindfulness. I will admit, sitting there in Quaama with my headphones on, to feeling like an adolescent student, all knees and elbows, on a tiny chair on a kindy classroom—'become aware of the sounds around you ... feel where you connect with your seat, your feet on the floor ...'. But the presenter was excellent—I can only describe her manner as 'calm exuberance'. I subdued my hubris and by the end of the presentation was convinced. I was ready.

Now I realise that meditation is key—to holding dark thoughts, fears of the future, at bay, and to maintaining a frame of mind that allows the calmest, strongest base to work from. And the work, from now on, is preserving the capacities I have, to stay independent and productive and happy.

* * *

I can still see electroencephalography recordings from my work at North Shore Medical Centre nearly thirty years ago. The alpha rhythm was dominant in a calm, focused mind; the faster beta rhythm indicated stress. Gamma waves, which I rarely recorded in my little room in St Leonards, are the highest frequency and are involved in higher mental acuity, including perception and consciousness. Meditation has been shown to decrease beta wave activity and to increase gamma activity.

Norman Doidge speaks of 'noisy brain'. Dysfunctional or injured neurons produce 'noise'—aberrant signals that make it harder for the true signals to be heard. And Doidge speaks of patients entering meditative states while using the PoNS.

In June 2016 I had a short stay in hospital with another attack of neuralgia. Again, the only drug that worked was the opiate Fentanyl, which I quickly realised I didn't want to continue. But I did make a discovery.

It's never dark or silent on a hospital ward at night. There's always dim light from the corridor, and muted, thin beams from nurses' torches. Occasional chimes from patient call buttons, followed by the soft squeak of rubber soles on linoleum, conversations of varying volume. The snuffles and rustlings of the room-mate behind the curtain.

I used these hours of wakefulness to work on a new technique.

I'd do a 'body scan'. I'd move my attention slowly from the tips of my toes up, resting on each part—the pad behind my toes, arch of the foot, heel, ankle ... lower back, waist, shoulder blades ... When I was truly focused I'd feel a mild sensation—a tingle or buzzing, a sprinkle of charged glitter. I'd pause and wait for this at each point. Then, by the time I reached the crown of my head, the pain would be gone. It's arduous, and it's not a solution; to hold the pain at bay I had to maintain concentration at that point, the crown, the tingle there increasing in intensity until it was almost an ache itself. Because as soon as my attention wavered ... whack! The pain would be back. The ultimate Zen master's stick.

It was only later, when I heard Richard Fidler's interview with Norman Doidge on Radio National in July 2016, that I learned that many pain-processing areas in the brain are closely associated with image-processing areas. Doidge said that if the brain is concentrating on processing imagery, there's less space for pain.

I think I'm onto something here. I can feel the confluence of Eastern mysticism and Western science in a neat dovetail: a quiet mind. And that's where I'm heading next.

But if peace of mind is what I was after, there was something I need to stare down first. Unfinished business.

***

I have a photo of Mum and Dad and me. It's dated simply '1966' on the back in Mum's neat hand; I look to be about three months old. It's summer and Mum and Dad are sitting on wickerwork chairs in our back yard in Violet Street, Mum in a cotton blouse, Dad in a polo shirt. I'm on Dad's lap. Mum reaches across

Dad, smiling, to hold my hand between her fingers. Dad's cradling me carefully with both hands and gazing down at me, head cocked, grinning.

This photo is in a collection that Jon put together for my fiftieth birthday. He asked Dad for the family albums to find the ones he wanted, and made it clear what he was doing, and why. My sister-in-law, Flavienne, fixed them with photo corners onto the craft paper pages of an ornate leather album.

There's another shot a couple of pages later: me, still a small baby, held aloft in two tanned, brawny arms. Another few pages later I'm about two, sponging the fender of an FH Holden, those same strong forearms scrubbing a headlight in the foreground. Later, a photo of the four of us, dated October '69—Jon was two, I was almost four. Dad's smiling, but not so broadly. The next one is dated May '71—I talked about this one earlier. Dad is sitting on a stone step, me beside him and Jon between his feet. Dad's elbows are on his knees, his hands clasped, and he's looking down. He's not smiling. There are no more photos of him in the album.

But now, at fifty, I turned to that first photo in the garden again and again. There was a time, although a brief one, when Dad looked pleased to be my father. I wondered if he remembered it. There was, I thought, one way to find out.

11. a message from fifty years ago

January 2016 and I was back in St Paul's Anglican Church. Last time I'd been there it was Mum's funeral in 2006 and the church was crowded but the air hushed and sombre. Now I was in the front pew again, and again there was a full house. But applause was rising around me—in the pews behind, up in the gallery, to the vaulted ceiling. There were whoops and cheers and whistles. Matt and Amber had made their vows and had turned to face the congregation. Their shy smiles turned to wide grins then laughter as the hearty show of appreciation, for them and their delayed nuptials, continued. And continued…

When my brother was twenty-five he told me he was determined to 'break the cycle'. For him, that meant not having children. It saddened me—I knew he would never be like Dad—but I understood. I had similar sentiments myself. Matt avoided intimate relationships until his early thirties, when he met Amber. And maybe it was those concerns that made him wait another nine years before asking this beautiful, kind music teacher to marry him. And on this afternoon in January 2016 I was delighted that he'd changed his mind.

Jon had married Flavienne in London when he was twenty-seven. They have three bright, happy, healthy children. I love being around their family—they talk, they help each other, they laugh together, they enjoy each other's company (I know I would have talked my young parents-to-be out of marrying, that night in the dining room on the *Willem Ruys*, but then the world would have been without Baptiste, Sébastien and Emeline). Jon certainly didn't turn into Dad. But he had the advantage of suffering Dad's neglect, rather than his spite. Maybe Dad was Jon's reverse role model for parenting.

That evening, after Matt's wedding at St Paul's, we gathered at a reception at Athol Hall on Bradleys Head, Mosman, to celebrate. It was a charming heritage venue but predated any awareness of disabled access. I found a seat on a small rise and sat to recover from my cross-country arrival. I watched the crowd, mostly smart, professional thirty- and forty-somethings, standing in small groups to drink champagne, chat and enjoy the twilight view over the indigo waters of Athol Bay to the gleaming sails of the Opera House and the Harbour Bridge beyond. It had been a perfect day for a wedding and the evening was warm and still.

From my vantage point I could see Dad, alone at the edge of the crowd, hands in pockets, contemplating the harbour. I imagined him reliving his days of piloting the *Macedon* through the deeper channels of these waterways. He didn't know any of Matt's friends and his relationship with much family present that day was strained. He'd met Amber and her parents only that afternoon.

As the evening deepened I was worried that Dad may decide to leave early and I'd miss my chance, so I asked my Auntie Karen to tell Dad that I'd like to talk to him. I'd told family members what I intended and reassured them—there would never be an occasion as safe as this one—but they were concerned.

Karen squeezed my shoulder and threaded her way through the crowd to Dad. It had the air of a summons, but I knew he'd be curious. I saw him glance at me, pause to take a glass of champagne from a passing waiter, then head over. Soon he was next to me. I only realised I'd been tense when my shoulders loosened; Dad wasn't the monolith of my memory, but a shorter, wizened version with rheumy eyes. He wore a tie with merchant navy insignia, and a peaked cap that looked vaguely nautical.

He started talking before he was fully seated. He asked me how I was, and what I'd been up to. He asked where I was living.

I blinked. 'In Quaama.'

He frowned. 'Where?'

'On the Far South Coast, near Bega. You've been there.'

He looked confused. After all we'd been through, the irony of that crossed my mind. But I wasn't there for that.

'Dad, I want to show you something.' I pulled the photo from my bag. 'Do you remember this?'

There we were again, Mum, Dad and me, on those wicker chairs in 1966, Dad holding me tenderly and gazing at me, smiling. Now, on a white plastic chair at Athol Hall, he pursed his lips and exhaled. 'Well, yes, that fence in the background there, you can see I was building that. I liked to save a dollar when I could, and I was pretty handy—'

'No, I mean, you're happy, aren't you? You look pretty happy to have me there, on your lap.' I tapped on the photo. His face, that grin. Auntie Karen wandered past, ostentatiously ignoring us.

Dad leaned back in his chair. 'Yes, you see, there's your mother. When you were about eleven you started getting a bit uppity, and your mother always took your side in things—'

'No, Dad.' I caught his gaze. 'Look at your face. I was just a baby. Were you happy to be my father?'

He looked down at the photo for a few seconds, then out across the darkening harbour. Lights were just starting to twinkle in the city. And for a moment in time, a curtain drew aside on another universe.

'You were magic…' he murmured.

For a moment.

I held my breath.

'But your mother, you see, she always thought you were in the right, all three of you kids, and I was in the wrong …'

I'd heard this before. He'd told me back in 1994, in that bright little sunroom, after the Hoffman Process. He'd been concerned that Mum's attitude would take a toll later, that the world out there was a hard place, that he should 'knock us down a peg or two' to prepare us. But now in 2016, I was only half listening. I'd been *magic*.

Then he was telling me about his properties, their valuations, his current net worth, the 'girlfriends' he'd had, the two women he was 'sizing up' on a dating website at the moment. 'You see, I'm eighty-three now. There aren't many men left, at my age, but there are still plenty of women …'

I realised I was getting bored. Auntie Julie drifted past and glanced at me quizzically. The band had started playing inside and Hansa had appeared at the doorway from time to time, peering out at us, eyebrows raised. The next time I saw him I waved and he made his way over. I quickly introduced him to Dad and we excused ourselves.

***

What had I wanted, that evening? I'm pretty clear about what I didn't want. I certainly didn't want a scene, not on Matt's day. I wasn't after an explanation, let alone an apology, for his legal actions. I didn't want or expect understanding, affection, friendship, any kind of promise for any kind of future. Reconciliation had no relevance for us. And there was too little time to build anything new, even if either of us had the inclination.

What I wanted was recognition. Acknowledgment of something … my daughterhood, for want of a less awkward word. That was what I saw in the photo. That would have been enough for me.

What did I get?

In the presence of my father, I felt calm, strong and powerful. I realised that Dad no longer frightened me. I didn't resent him. I didn't love him or even like him. I felt completely neutral. He could have been any old man, come to deliver a message—a message from fifty years ago.

When I think back about that night, Dad was the tanned young man in the wicker seat, beaming at me, not the old man in a sailor cap, griping and obfuscating in the white plastic chair. Just for an instant, we cut through fifty years of resentment, anger, fear and disappointment, to a time of untarnished love. I'd been a daughter, a cherished daughter.

When I left him to go inside with Hansa, I thanked him and said goodbye. No hug, no kiss; we didn't so much as shake hands. I wasn't sure if I would see that old man again. But it didn't matter—he was just a messenger.

***

I've come to the conclusion lately that there's no such thing as *what really happened*. There's just present-day memories. Of my childhood, there's my memory and Dad's memory. What really happened no longer exists.

Then there was what happened that January evening in 2016, on two plastic chairs in the sultry twilight on the foreshores of Athol Bay, strains of jazz and clinking glasses, laughter and chatter in the background. And even aspects of that have taken on the mutable cast of memory.

But of one thing I'm sure. He said it. I was magic.

***

'Have you ever considered you might have got the MS because you can't forgive your dad?'

There are many, many theories about what causes MS but after years of my own research I suspect that my immune system was brought low by a weakened microbiome. MS is an inflammatory process, and gut flora regulate inflammation. Frequent courses of antibiotics as a child, and that prolonged course prior to my kidney operation when I was twenty, would have contributed to enfeebled gut flora.

But chronically high stress hormone (cortisol) levels during my first twenty years wouldn't have helped—high cortisol has also been shown to affect immune development. Giulia Enders, in *Gut* (2015) writes that in children the 'gut brain' develops in line with the 'head brain'; stress at mealtime activates nerves that inhibit digestion. Mealtimes were the only times when our family gathered—and the scene of almost nightly conflicts, or the dreaded anticipation of them, when Dad was home. The eczema, if that's what those sticky lesions on my fifteen-year-old fingers were, was just a small physical manifestation of the anxiety inside.

Recently, frustrated with months of insomnia and daytime drowsiness, I mentioned my woes to my

GP. She arranged a twenty-four hour salivary cortisol test. The results came back to show that instead of peaking in the early morning and declining gradually until bedtime, my cortisol was flat-lining in the medium range throughout. In other words it was too high at night, keeping me awake, and too low during the day, explaining my lethargy.

'Stage Three Adrenal Exhaustion,' announced Lily, looking at the graph.

'Wow,' I said. 'What does Stage Four look like?'

'There *is* no Stage Four,' she said.

It seems that life-long high cortisol levels have brought me to this in my middle age, and Western medicine has no answer. I'm seeing a self-reinforcing loop here. High cortisol brings on autoimmune disease, which itself causes long term stress.

But as for my initial susceptibility to MS, there must have been another factor, or factors, otherwise there'd be an MS epidemic in the Western world. Research implicates genetics, and environmental factors such as infections (perhaps Epstein Barr virus—glandular fever—which I contracted as a teenager). Recently, mainstream medicine has suggested that low Vitamin D levels could be a cause—something that George Jelinek wrote about as early as 1999. We spent summers at the beach, as kids, but Mum was always very careful about sun-hats and sunscreen.

Perhaps I was tossed and battered by the perfect storm, only one tempestuous element of which was Dad.

* * *

In November 2015 I held a party at the Quaama Hall for my fiftieth birthday. I invited seventy guests, including family, my co-workers from the *Triangle*, Quaama friends and neighbours, and of course my big, rowdy sannyas family. I hired a couple of musicians that I've admired for many years, a caterer who does a great vegetarian spread, and a cake-maker to do something gluten-free, dairy-free and delicious.

I put all this in place. Then, being me, I worried about all the things that could go wrong. Musicians get laryngitis, caterers get food poisoning, guests don't show…

But it was a wonderful night. Jon was between treatments and feeling well, and he, Flavienne and their kids, who'd driven down from Sydney the day before, decorated the Hall with Hansa's sister Mary and brother-in-law John; it looked glorious. When I arrived at 7 pm there was already quite a crowd there and they kept pouring in. The food, a 'Mediterranean Feast', was delectable; the music a perfect mix of soulful dinner accompaniment and jivey dance for afterwards; the cake a liqueur-infused chocolate mousse cake with a tumble of berries—need I say more?

After the dinner and cake were done, I sat for a while watching the dance floor. There was my ubercool seventeen-year-old nephew, Baptiste, busting rap moves and swinging ten-year-old Emeline around. My writing partner, Sarah, and Linda from the *Triangle* team shimmied around each other to *Mustang Sally*. Bruce and Julie from the gym bopped to *Foxy Lady*. And all the time my sannyasin tribe, spinning and bouncing around with joy and abandon to anything being played.

When Santana's *Smooth* came on, late into the night, even I had a bit of a dance—in Hansa's arms. Then, pooped, I sank into a chair and looked around the crowd. Everyone there was a special part of my life, most from the life I'd made myself here in Quaama. And everyone who was special in my life, with just a handful of exceptions, was there with me that night.

As I sat there I realised something else, and it had started when the crowd sang 'Happy Birthday'. There was a funny moment at the end of the third line when half sang 'Happy birthday, dear Jen' and the other half sang 'Happy birthday, dear Sahi', and with a little start I realised that I'd done it. Perhaps in the line of that song it jarred a little, and there were a few laughs, but that just underscored for me that finally, after twenty-eight years, I'd merged my two existences, my two names, my two lives.

There in our little community hall I felt a strong sense of having arrived—having arrived where I belong.

June 2017. Hansa and I arrive in the oncology ward at Royal North Shore Hospital. Jon's been admitted again and this time it's hard to imagine he'll be coming out.

The manuscript of this book is in my bag, a hardcopy I just got back from the editor. Jon's been wanting to read it for the last year but I've been putting him off. His scans have been good, it wasn't really ready and it felt like there was all the time in the world ... But suddenly his scans aren't good anymore and I realise I've left it too late. I've marked some pages with post-it notes, those parts I really want to share with him. Driving up the coast today I've imagined sitting by his bedside, reading to him as he drifts in and out of consciousness.

I find Room 25, steel myself and peer through the glass window in the door. Jon's sitting up in bed, doing a crossword.

He's on a morphine pump and the pain is under control to some degree, he says. I pull the manuscript out and he says, 'Great! I'd love to read it.' It's my only copy of my editor's comments and scribbles so I hesitate ... briefly. 'Of course,' I say. I leave it with him that day.

Jon gets to Chapter Six before reading becomes too tiring. Flavienne passes on some of his comments and corrections to me.

I last see Jon two weeks later. Hansa and I are at the Greenwich hospice. We're ordering a Thai takeaway dinner for everyone and ask him if he has any requests. 'Anything with cashews,' he says, smiling. Flavienne's there too, and the children, and Caramelle, their beloved Golden Retriever, and Jon's full of smiles that night: soft, tender smiles.

'Until next time,' he tells me when I lean over to kiss him goodbye. He dies two days later, on 21 June.

On 19 July, a child is born to Matt and Amber. A beautiful girl, Naomi Elise. Matt is smitten. Soon he leaves work to be a stay-at-home dad.

And me? My MS has progressed a little more. I use a walker almost all the time now, and my hands are shakier. But Hansa and I are coping; we continue to adjust. We're managing—I just can't afford to get any worse …

Long Road to Dry River

With Dad and the FH, 1967

With Jon and Matt, Violet Street, 1973

With Mum, Blue Mountains, 1992

With Matt, Flavienne and Jon, London, 1996

Flavienne, me, Matt, Jon, Grandpa, Sangrado Street, Christmas 1997

In the garden in Quaama, 1998

With Hansa, 2009

With Matt and Jon at Matt and Amber's wedding, 2016

Acknowledgments

Thanks to MS Australia for the Go for Gold Scholarship that allowed me to engage life-writing mentor Rae Luckie. To Rae for lessons in accessing memories and bringing text to life. To Peter Shepherd for his incredible, life-affirming writing classes—and to my fellow students. To Mary Cunnane for her encouragement from the early stages and her invaluable advice throughout. To my readers—Annabel Blay, Rose Chaffey, Sarah Gardiner, Ian McFarlane, Heather O'Connor and Tikka Wilson—for their various insights and suggestions. And to Rose, too, for allowing me to use her beautiful watercolour on the cover. To Julie Daniel, my aunt, for pointing out what this book is really about. And to Hansa, for his steadfast love and support, and for making my life so much easier than it might have been.

Bibliography

- *The Tongue-Tip Taste of Tao*, Rajneesh Foundation, 1981
- *Overcoming Multiple Sclerosis: The Evidence-Based 7 Step Recovery Program*, George Jelinek, 2016
- *The Wahls Protocol: A Radical New Way to Treat All Chronic Autoimmune Conditions Using Paleo Principles*, Terry Wahls and Eve Adamson, 2015
- *The Brain that Changes Itself*, Norman Doidge, 2010
- *The Brain's Way of Healing*, Norman Doidge, 2015
- *Gut: The Inside Story of Our Body's Most Underrated Organ*, Giulia Enders, 2015

www.ingramcontent.com/pod-product-compliance
Lightning Source LLC
Chambersburg PA
CBHW020857110526
R18273100001B/R182731PG44587CBX00003B/5